미래를 빛낼 시인들의
국영문 시선집

Anthology of Korean Poets
for the Shining Future in Korean/English

미래를 빛낼 시인들의
국영문 시선집

Anthology of Korean Poets
for the Shining Future in Korean/English

순 수

◆ 발간사

우리 말에 담긴 한국인의 정신

朴 永 河

  고 박태진 시인께서는 프랑스에서 공부하셨고 오랫동안 그곳에서 생활하셨습니다. 그러나 생전에 시인은 국내 독자들에게 외국의 문학 사조를 소개함으로서 한국문학의 질적 향상을 위하여 활발한 활동을 하셨습니다. 시인의 영향하에 1995년에 제 개인 시집을 영역하여 출간한 일도 있었습니다. 그 이후 순수 문학 출판사는 노벨문학상 수상자를 비롯하여 세계 여러 유명 시인들의 시를 한국어 뿐만 아니라 영어와 프랑스어로 출판해 왔습니다. 1997년과 1998년에 외국 유명 시인들의 작품을 한글로 번역하여 국내 서점에 배포하여, 이들 시인들의 훌륭한 문학적 비젼을 국내 독자들에게 소개하였습니다. 이를 통하여 국내의 문학 독자와 작가들이 외국의 문학과 문화를 경험할 수 있었다고 믿습니다.

2000년 대에 들어서 국내의 많은 출판사들이 한국 시를 영어, 일본어, 프랑스어, 독일어 그리고 중국어로 번역하여 출판하기 시작하였고, 출판된 시집들을 전 세계 여러 서점에 배포하였습니다. 한국문학을 외국에 소개하기 위한 국내 출판사들의 이러한 노력은 요즈음 유행하는 한류에서 한국문학의 인기 상승에서 그 결과를 찾아볼 수 있다고 생각합니다.

  우리는 지금 과거에 경험해 보지 못했던 새로운 사회적 환경에서 생활하고 있습니다. 우리는 다양한 이유로 한국에 온 다민족 이주민들과 한국어와 한국 문화를 배우고자 한국에 온 외국 학생들과 함께 생활하는 시대를 살아가고 있는 것입니다. 이러한 환경에서 보다 많은 한국시를 다양한 언어로 번역하고 출판하여, 우리 언어 속에 담겨 있는 한국인의 정신을 세계인들에게 소개하는 일이 더욱 중요해졌습니다. 그것이 바로 제가 이 시집을 출간하기로 결정한 이유입니다, 이 시집을 출간 할 수 있도록 소중한 원고들을 보내주신 여러 시인들에게 진심으로 감사드립니다. 또한 시 시집에 수록된 작품들의 대다수를 번역해준 김인영 박사님께 감사드립니다.

한국문인협회 시분과 회장 / 月刊 순수문학 편집주간

◆Publishing Announcement

The Spirits of Korean People Embedded in Our Language, Hangeul

Park Young-Ha

Late poet Park Tae-jin studied in France and stayed there for a long time. But when he was still alive, he actively participated in improving Korean literature by introducing foreign literary trends to the literary readers in Korea. Under his influence, I had published a collection of my poems translated into English in 1995. Since then, the publishing company Seonsoo Literature has been publishing the collections of poems written by the Nobel Prize winners and renowned poets around the world not only in Korean but also in English and French. In 1997 and 1998 we published many poetry books of foreign poets translated into Korean and distributed them to the book stores in Korea in order to introduce the great literary visions of those famous poets. And the literary readers and writers in Korea were pleased to experience the literary culture of foreign countries.

Since the year 2000 or so, many literary publishers in Korea began to release Korean poetry books translated into different languages such as English, Japanese, French, German and Chinese and distributed them to the bookstore worldwide. The efforts these publishers have made to introduce Korean literature to the foreign readers are now getting results as we can see from the increasing popularity of K-Literature.

These days, we are living in a new social environment that we haven't experienced before. I mean, we are living with multi-ethnic families who came to Korea for various reasons and also with many foreign students who came to Korea to learn our language and culture. Under these circumstances, it has become more important to publish more Korean poetry translated into different languages and make the people around the world know the spirits of Korean people embedded in our language. That's why we have decided to publish this collection of poems. I appreciate those poets who contributed their poems for the publication. And I'l like to thank Dr. Kim In-young who translated most of the poems included in this collection.

Chairperson of Poetry Division in The Korean Writers Association & Editor-in-chief of monthly magazine Seonsoo Literature

발간사/朴永河·4

강호남	교차	외 1편/ 14
고종호	꽃샘추위	외 1편/ 22
김경희	못난이 유원지	외 1편/ 26
김남성	살구 꽃	외 1편/ 30
김명돌	태양은 하루만 산다	외 1편/ 34
김봉렬	내 마음	외 1편/ 40
김선영	오랜 이별 끝에서	외 1편/ 44
김선진	꿈꾸는 꽃	외 1편/ 48
김윤준	가을날	외 1편/ 52
김현신	바람이 늙어갑니다	외 1편/ 58
김혜원	여린 봄	외 1편/ 62
남종구	빛의 세월	외 1편/ 66
문순심	고향 유정	외 1편/ 70
문영현	통영 아침노을	외 1편/ 76
문 웅	질그릇 같은 세월	외 1편/ 84
박경임	초록피	외 1편/ 88
박순자	영산강	외 1편/ 92
朴永河	석류꽃	외 1편/ 98
박완순	시, 공간 초월	외 1편/ 102
박종권	대청봉	외 1편/ 110

Publishing Announcement/Park Young-Ha · 6

Kang Ho-Nam	Crossing etc/15
Go Jong-Ho	The Cold Snap etc/23
Gim Gyeong-Hui	Retro Corner for Oldies but Goodies etc/27
Kim Nam-Sung	Apricot Blossoms etc/31
Kim Myung-Dol	The Sun Lives Only a Day etc/35
Kim Bong-Ryul	My Mind etc/41
Kim Seon-Yeong	Long After A Breakup etc/45
Kim Sun-Jin	A Dreaming Flower etc/49
Kim Yoon-Jun	An Autumn Day etc/53
Kim Hyun-Shin	The Wind Getting Old etc/59
Kim He-Won	In Delicate Spring etc/63
Nam Jong-Gu	Time Passing So Fast Like Light etc/67
Moon Soon-Sim	Love and Affection for My Hometown etc/71
Moon Young-Hyun	The Morning Glow in Tongyoung etc/77
Moon Woong	Time like Unglazed Pottery etc/85
Park Kyung-Im	Green Blood etc/89
Park Soon-Ja	Youngsan River etc/93
Park Young-Ha	Flower of Pomegranate etc/99
Park Oane-Soon	Transcending Time and Space etc/103
Park Jong-Kwun	Daecheongbong Peak etc/111

박종흡	여명(黎明) 외 1편/ 114
박철언	바람의 언덕에서 외 1편/ 118
박희정	기다린 봄 외 1편/ 122
방안나	국화처럼 외 1편/ 126
백점숙	유빙 외 1편/ 132
서상문	사랑의 의미 외 1편/ 138
소명환	노모님과 함께 외 1편/ 142
소융일	엄마의 강 외 1편/ 146
손준식	삼월 거리에 나서면 외 1편/ 150
송낙현	섬 외 1편/ 154
오정선	시를 읽는 소녀 외 1편/ 158
오종민	레테 외 1편/ 162
오현정	오늘 외 1편/ 166
유장희	격랑(激浪) 외 1편/ 170
윤수자	봄날의 편지 외 1편/ 178
윤주홍	가을 無題(무제) 외 1편/ 182
윤호용	다섯 손가락 외 1편/ 186
이금희	편지 외 1편/ 194
이행자	썩고지고 죽고지고 외 1편/ 202
이현채	진달래 피었구나 외 1편/ 206

Park Jong-Heup	At Dawn etc/ 115	
Park Chul-Un	On the Hill of Wind etc/ 119	
Park Hee-Jung	Spring We Have Been Waiting For etc/ 123	
Bang An-Na	Like Chrysanthemums etc/ 127	
Baik Jeum-Sook	Drift Ice etc/ 133	
Suh Sang-Mun	The meaning of love etc/ 139	
So Myung-Hwan	With My Old Mother etc/ 143	
So Yung-Il	Mother's River etc/ 147	
Son Jun-Shik	Coming out to the Streets of March etc/ 151	
Song Nak-Hyun	An Island etc/ 155	
Oh Jeong-Seon	A Girl Reading a Poem etc/ 159	
Oh Jong-Min	Lethe etc/ 163	
Oh Hyun-Jung	Today etc/ 167	
Yoo Jang-Hee	Heavy Seas etc/ 171	
Yoon Sou-Ja	A Letter of the Spring etc/ 179	
Yoon Ju-Hong	Autumn Untitled etc/ 183	
Yun Ho-Yong	Five Fingers etc/ 187	
Lee Keum-Hee	A Letter etc/ 195	
Lee Haeng-Ja	Turning to Dust Again In the Holy Spirit etc/ 203	
Lee Hyun-Chae	Azaleas Blooming etc/ 207	

임병숙	멋진 노년의 미소	외 1편/ 210
정도병	굿샷	외 1편/ 214
정연수	강릉 커피	외 1편/ 222
조대연	비워 내림	외 1편/ 226
조앵순	소망	외 1편/ 234
조풍연	피안彼岸 길	외 1편/ 238
주광일	박꽃	외 1편/ 242
채자경	새해의 기도	외 1편/ 246
최예찬	할미꽃	외 1편/ 250
최외득	맞바람	외 1편/ 254
최철훈	광음(光陰)	외 1편/ 258
추정희	향기에 취해	외 1편/ 262
하재룡	라일락꽃 피면	외 1편/ 266
한민서	제자리	외 1편/ 270
한현삼	환희	외 1편/ 274
홍경자	일을 하는 마음	외 1편/ 278
홍금희	첫눈 오는 날	외 1편/ 282
홍영숙	봄날의 조우	외 1편/ 290
홍은숙	무덤	외 1편/ 294

Im Byung-Sook	Beautiful Smiles at Old Age etc/ 211
Jung Do-Byung	Good Shot etc/ 215
Jeong Yeon-Soo	Gangneung Coffee etc/ 223
Cho Dae-Yeun	Emptying Down etc/ 227
Cho Aeng-Sun	A Hope etc/ 235
Cho Poong-Youn	The Path for Nirvana etc/ 239
Chu Kwang-Il	Gourd flower etc/ 243
Chae Ja-Kyung	A Prayer for the New Year etc/ 247
Choi Yea-Chan	Pasqueflower etc/ 251
Choi Woe-Deuk	Headwind etc/ 255
Choi Cheul-Hoon	The Fleeting Light and Shadow etc/ 259
Chu Jeong-Hee	Intoxicated in the Scent etc/ 263
Ha Jai-Ryong	If Lilacs bloom etc/ 267
Han Min-Seo	The Same Place etc/ 271
Han Hyun-Sam	Joy etc/ 275
Hong Kyung-Ja	The Mind at Work etc/ 279
Hong Geum-Hee	On the Day the First Snow Falls etc/ 283
Hong Young-Sook	An Encounter of a Spring Day etc/ 291
Hong Eun-Sug	Graves etc/ 295

강호남

교차

일점오미터 풀에 양손 끝을 모아 정수리부터 몸을 던진다
뜨거운 남국의 태양 아래서 속초 돌섬 감싼 검푸른 바다를
만나러 간다

물속으로 들어가며 만들어진 물의 저항은
건너오던 물결의 파동과 만나고
그녀의 검은 수경은 나를 잠시 바라보더니
이내 바닥을 보며 가던 길을 간다

그녀가 코에서 뿜어낸 굵은 숨 방울들이
수면을 향해 부상하던 나의 뺨에 와 닿는다

의식하지 못한 근육질의 어깨를 지나치는 동안
그녀가 만든 파동의 울림이 내가 만드는 파동의 울림과
섞이는 것을 느꼈다

Kang Ho-Nam

Crossing

I put my hands together in the one-point-five meter
pool and throw myself in from the top of my head
I go to meet the dark blue sea surrounding Sokcho
Rock Island under the hot southern sun

The resistance of the water created as I go into the
water
meets the waves of the waves that were crossing
Her black glasses look at me for a moment
and then continue on her way looking at the bottom

The thick bubbles of breath she exhaled from her nose
touch my cheek as I rise toward the surface

While passing by the muscular shoulders that I was
not aware of
I felt the echo of the waves she made mixing with the
echo of the waves I made

그제야 나는 나의 숨 방울들을 수면 위로 뱉어내며
시간과 공간의 만남이라는 것은 파동과 숨결의 만남이라는 것과
참 많이 닮았다고 생각했다

〈서울문학〉 시인 등단. 〈순수문학〉 수필가 등단. 연세대학교 도시공학 박사, 성균관대학교 경영학 석사, 연세대학교 건축공학 학사. 건축시공기술사. 서경대학교 융합대학원 겸임교수. 시집 〈야간비행〉. 저서 〈웰쓰 엔지니어링〉

Only then did I spit out my bubbles of breath above the surface
and thought that the meeting of time and space is very similar
to the meeting of waves and breath

〈Seoul Literature〉 Poet Debut. 〈Pure Literature〉 Essayist Debut. PhD in Urban Planning and Engineering from Yonsei University. Master of Business Administration from Sungkyunkwan University. Bachelor of Architecture and Architectural Engineering from Yonsei University. Professional Engineer of Architectural Construction. Adjunct Professor at the Graduate School of Convergence, Seokyeong University. Poetry Collection 〈Night Flight〉. Book 〈Wealth Engineering〉

강호남

만남

머물지 못하는 사월의 꽃잎처럼 시간은 너를 지나친다
번호표 하나 주지 않고 형체 없는 몸으로 바람처럼
밀어낸다
조금씩 떨어지는 비가 마침내 대지를 삼키듯
한 올씩 쌓인 시간은 한껏 너를 삼킨다

차가운 저녁을 밝히는 천만 개의 등불 꺼진 나의 인연은 어디
에도 보이지 않는다
어지러운 군중들이 스르르 열어준 정확한 이정표처럼
우연을 반복하다 서서히 드러난 필연의 운명처럼
걸어가야 할 길은 명확하다

Kang Ho-Nam

Encounter

Like the flower petals of April that can't stay, time passes you by
Without giving you a single number, it pushes you away like the wind with its formless body
Just as the rain that falls little by little finally swallows the earth
Time, piled up one by one, swallows you whole

My fate, which has been turned off by the tens of millions of lights that brighten the cold evening, is nowhere to be seen
Like the precise milestones that the dizzying crowd gently opens
Like the inevitable fate that gradually reveals itself through repeated coincidences
The path I must take is clear

문 앞의 소포처럼 너에게로 갔다 수신인의 서명을 받지 못하고도

삼월 바닷가의 유채꽃처럼 쓸쓸한 환영을 기대한다

너는 항상 나의 밖에 있다 시간은 너와의 대면을 허락하지 않는다

그렇다 해도 너를 삼킨 시간은 결국 떠날 것이다

나는 너를 알 수 있다 너도 나를 알 수 있다

장미가 만개할 무렵에는 맨발로 나오는 너를 만날 것이다

I went to you like a parcel in front of the door
Without receiving the recipient's signature
I expect a lonely welcome like rape blossoms on the beach in March
You are always outside of me. Time does not allow me to face you
Even so, the time that swallowed you will eventually leave

I can know you, and you can know me too
When the roses are in full bloom, I will meet you coming out barefoot

고종호

꽃샘추위

꽃샘추위에 정원의 꽃들이
와들와들 떨고 고개를 숙이지만

이 추위를 견디고 일어서야
짙고 아름다운 색깔의 꽃을 피운다.

동두천 출생. 건국대학교 국어국문학과, 대진대학교 국어 교육학과 대학원 졸업. 월간 순수문학으로 등단. 2022년 순수문학 우수상 수상, 교사로 정년퇴임, 홍조근정훈장, 연천 청산에서 농부로 생활함.

Go Jong-Ho

The Cold Snap

Flower buds in the garden lower their heads
Trembling in a cold snap

Overcoming the spell of cold weather
To bring forth flowers in rich and beautiful colors

Retired teacher. B.A majoring in Korean literature from Konkuk Univ. & M.A in Korean education from Daejin Graduate School. Made literary debut through *Seonsoo Literature* in 2022. Awarded Seonsoo Literature Prize & Order of Service Merit Red Stripes.

고종호

반딧불이

어둑어둑 어둠이 몰려온 저녁
유리창에 반짝이는 작은 빛이 어른거린다

다가가 보니 반딧불이 한 마리가 날아와선
유리창에 붙어 원을 그리며 춤을 춘다

아! 얼마 만인가? 저편 넘어 기억 속 반딧불이

어릴적 여름밤엔 흔케 군무(群舞)하며 춤추던 반딧불이
지금은 가끔 어쩌다가 볼 수 있으니

장마가 한숨 쉬고 있는 사이
반딧불이를 만나 어릴적 추억으로 데려간다

이 흔한 추억을 기억할 수 있는 사람이 얼마나 남았을지
사람들이 편하고 쉬운 것만 찾다 보니 반딧불이가
사라진 것은 아닐지

지구가 아파 아름다운 추억까지도 아픈 것은 아닐지.

Go Jong-Ho

Glowworm

In the evening gradually getting darker and darker
a twinkling light appears shimmering on the window

Getting closer to the window where a glow-worm has flown down
I find it dancing around, making a circle

Ah! How long has passed since I kept glow-worms in my mind

In youth I used to see glowworms dancing in group at summer nights
but now I can see them only by chance at times

At short breaks during monsoon
the glowworms I get a glimpse of take me back to my childhood

I wonder how many people are left to remem-ber the good old days;
we might have made glowworms mostly dis-appear for our own sake

The earth in pain makes our beautiful me-mories of the past much more painful

김경희

못난이 유원지

입장권 한 장으로
옛 시간을 살 수 있을까

삐걱거리는 계단 따라
희미한 불빛 따라

오란씨 한병
라면땅 하나
해진 교복도 정겹고

빛바랜 사진 한 장
사무치는 날

헤이리,
못난이 유원지에 가보고 싶다

충청남도 천안 출생. 2021년「純粹文學」현대시로 등단. 2024년 공저:「시의 사계」, 「시작이 반이다, 다시 시작이다」. 한국문인협회원.

Gim Gyeong-Hui

Retro Corner for Oldies but Goodies

With an admission ticket only
Is it possible to buy old times?

Walking on the squeaky stairs
Following a dim light

Enjoying various items on display such as a bottle of sparkling citrus,
a bag of Ramen snack, a worn out school uni-form,
all looking warm and familiar

On a day I miss the good old days so much
being reminded from a faded photograph

I long for visiting
Retro Corner for Oldies but Goodies in Heyri

Member of The Korean Writers Association. Made literary debut through *Seonsoo Literature* in 2021. Co-author of poetry books *Four Seasons of Poetry & Beginning is Half of the Whole, Now It's Another Beginning*

김경희

국수마을

허름한 간판
여덟 개 남짓 탁자
추억 한 그릇을 기다리는 사람들

벽에 걸린
뒷모습이 허전한 사람들과
국수가 먹고 싶다는
어느 시인의 시 한 편

콩국수 한 그릇
속타는 마음 식히고
잔치국수 한 그릇
눈물을 삼키고

비좁고 낡은 집에
저마다의 사연 털어놓고 가는
그 집, 고향마을

Gim Gyeong-Hui

A Town for Noodles

Shabby signboards
Eight tables casually set up
People waiting for a bowl of noodles with their memories

A poem hanging on the wall says
The poet wants to eat a bowl of noodles
Together with other people
Whose look from behind appears empty

With a bowl of bean noodles
Some people cool down their agitated mind
With a bowl of banquet noodles
Other people fight back tears

At a little cramped old house
People get their own stories off the chest
Before leaving
The place, their home town

김남성

살구꽃

아론의 지팡이 땅에 꽂았더니
움이 돋고 순이 나 꽃이 피어
살구 열매 맺어
생명의 기적을 보였네

하얀 꽃잎 아래 사랑의 열매
송알 송알 익어
순수한 믿음 어둠을 뚫고
빛이 되어

어지러운 세상에 희망의
메시지를 전하니
모두의 마음에
성령의 꽃 활짝 피기를

월간 순수 문학 시부문 등단. 순수 문학 회원. 성북 문창 회원. 월천 문학 동인 회원.
동인지 간이역 제13집-제15집

Kim Nam-Sung

Apricot Blossoms

When Aaron's rod was placed inside the Holiest place
the rod brought forth budding sprouts and flowers
growing to produce apricots,
manifesting miracles of life

Fruits of love under white petals
grow ripe in clusters
to bear innocent beliefs
that create light defeating the darkness

Delivering the message of hope
to us living in the world confusing and dis-orderly
promising the full blooming of the Holy Spirit
to the humble mind of us all

Member of Seonsoo Literature Association & Sungbuk Creative Writing. Made literary debut through *Seonsoo Literature*. Participation in Publishing literary coterie magazine, *A Halt Station* (volume 13-15)

김남성

첫눈

하늘에서 눈송이
살랑살랑 내려온다
첫눈은 약속처럼 찾아와
마음을 설레게 하고

세상의 더러움 잠시 나마
하얀 카펫을 깔고
야웅이 병정들 발자욱을 남긴다

밤이면 눈사람 걸어 다니며
눈송이들과 수다를 떨고
술래놀이를 할 것 같아

오늘 밤 나도 그들과 춤을 추며
모든 걱정 잠재우고 하얀 세상 속에
나를 새겨 넣는다

Kim Nam-Sung

The First Snow

Snowflakes blow down
from the sky gently
As if promised, the first snow comes down
making my heart flutter softly

On the white carpet laid
over the dirt of the world
only the footprints of cat soldiers are left

On the night of snow falling down
a snowman seems to walk around having a chat
or playing hide-and-seek with flurry snow-flakes

Tonight, I dance around in snow
letting all the worries off the chest
having myself engraved in the world of white snow

김명돌

태양은 하루만 산다

태양은 하루만 산다
어제의 태양은 오늘의 태양이 아니다
반복되는 똑같은 하루는 없다
똑같은 두 번의 아침도 없고
똑같은 두 번의 밤도 없다
똑같은 두 번의 노래도 없고
똑같은 두 번의 입맞춤도 없다
어제의 나가 오늘의 나가 아니듯
어제의 네가 오늘의 네가 아니다
태양이 하루를 빛나게 살듯이
하루하루를 소중하게 여기고
즐겁고 보람 있게 살아야 한다
매일 새롭게 태어나는 태양처럼
인생도 날마다 새로이 시작한다

경영학박사 목회학석사. 도보여행작가 광교세무법인 대표세무사 용인YMCA 이사장. 2017년 순수문학 등단.

Kim Myung-Dol

The Sun Lives Only a Day

The sun lives only a day
The sun of yesterday is not the same one today.
Such a day repeating all the same doesn't exist.
No morning exists repeating the same twice;
No evening exists repeating the same twice.
No song can be sung the same twice;
No kiss can be felt the same twice.
As if I am not the same me of yesterday
You are not the same one of yesterday.
As the sun shines to the end of a daytime
We should live a meaningful life as pleasantly as possible
Cherishing every single day of our life.
Like the sun rising afresh at every dawn
We should make everyday of our life a fresh start

Ph. D. in business administration. M.A. in pastoral theology. Made literary debut through *Seonsoo Literature* in 2017. Walking tour writer. Representative accountant of Gwang Kyo Tax Corporation. President of Yongin YMCA.

김명돌

나는 자유다

태산이 높다하되
하늘 아래 뫼이로다 했건만
한라산 백록담에 올랐을 때
중국 태산은 눈 아래 있었고
백두산 천지에 올랐을 때
한라산은 눈 아래 있었다
일본 후지산에 올랐을 때
백두산은 눈 아래 있었고
안나푸르나 베이스캠프에 올랐을 때
후지산은 눈 아래 있었다
중국 옥룡설산에 올랐을 때
안나푸르나 베이스캠프는 눈 아래 있었고
킬리만자로 우후르 피크에 올랐을 때
옥룡설산은 눈 아래 있었다

Kim Myung-Dol

I am Free

No matter how high Mount Tai in China is
it's just a mountain under the sky
Climbing up Mountain Halla with Baekrokdam crater
I felt like I could then look down at Mount Tai;
standing on top of Mountain Baekdu with the crater lake
I felt like I could then look down at Mountain Halla.
Climbing up Mountain Fuji in Japan
I felt like I could then look down at Mountain Baekdu;
standing at the Annapurna Base Camp
I felt like I could then look down at Mountain Fuji.
Climbing up Jade Dragon Snow Mountain in China
I felt like I could then look down at the Anna-purna Base Camp;
standing at the Uhuru Peak of Kilimanjaro
I felt like I could then look down at Jade Dra-gon Snow Mountain.
As if longing to be flying Jonathan Seagull that can see far away

높이 나는 조나단이 멀리 보듯이
하늘 아래 우뚝 솟은 정상을 향해
한 걸음 한 걸음 오를 때마다
사방팔방 펼쳐지는 아름다운 세상
'나는 자유다!'
유유자적 흰 구름이 흘러간다.

I climb up higher and higher at every step
towards the mountain top soaring high up under the sky
watching the world stretching out beautifully all around us
'I am free!' I said
feeling like I am a white cloud floating in peace

김봉렬

내 마음

산모롱이에 아지랑이 피어오르면
나의 마음은 연둣빛 고요
찰랑찰랑 윤슬 가득한 호반에
고사리손 흔들리는 작은 북소리에도
싱거웁게 미동하는 버드나무요

이른 봄날 스적스적 솔바람 불어
나의 낡은 영혼 구만리창공에
잠시간 머물다 인연 따라 떠나는
쓰르렁한 버들피리 한 곡조
봄 밭갈이 하는 양떼구름이 되어

하얀 모란꽃잎 온종일 산울림으로
흔들어 대는 바람의 언덕에서
봄비 맞은 버들가지 아래
여린 손가락 무심히 깍지를 끼고
후익후익 휘파람 불며 가리.

Kim Bong-Ryul

My Mind

The heat haze rises from the spur of the mountains
making my mind calm and placid in light green;
at the lake full of rippling waves
even soft sounds of drumbeat made by a cute little hand
let my mind sway like willow twigs rustling in the air

On a day in early spring the breeze blowing from the pine forest
makes my poor old soul briefly stay in the sky high and endless
before it leaves, following its own destiny in tune with willow flute,
to be part of cumulus clouds over the spring field being plowed

On the hill of the wind I can hear all day long
the echo of the mountains shaking white peony blossoms;
after having interlaced my feeble fingers
under the willow twigs soaked in spring rain
I am going to depart whistling a tune softly to myself

김봉렬

바람에게

한량없이 청징한 탐라의 바람아

원시의 사려니 숲길 가는 노루목

거문오름 거푸거푸 넘어가는 바람아

애써 가꾼 돌담길 넘어지지 않도록

마그마가 벌겋게 달궈지고 또 익어도

너는 나에게 다독다독 위로를 주었지

한라산 갈까마귀 무등 타는 바람아

간난 세월 이겨 낸 참빗 같은 구상나무

흰 사슴의 마른 눈빛도 닦아 주고 가려무나.

필(筆)동인 순수문학회 회원, 한국문인협회 회원, 향수옥천 회원, 창작과 비평 시요일 회원. 월간(月刊)순수문학 2022년 신인상 당선.수상 : 전국정지용백일장 입상. 작품집 : 한국문인협회 시분과 사화집 _"집"(2023), "시(詩)의 사계(四季)"(2024) 필(筆)동인지 공동시집 _제18집 "세월의 바람, 풀꽃 흔들며"(월간순수문학출판부),제19집 "시작이 반이다, 다시 시작이다"(월간순수문학출판부)

Kim Bong-ryul

To the Wind

The wind of Jeju Island so much clean and pure blows again and again
over the paths roe deer are frequently spotted near the forest trails
and over the Geomun Oreums, small rising extinct volcanoes on the island.

Keeping safe the stone wall I built with efforts not to be collapsing
soothing my suffering from magma burning hot inside me
you have always given me comforts

The wind blowing on the wings of ravens flying around Mountain Halla!
Stroke fir trees having a look of fine-tooth comb to overcome hard times
and make the dry eyes of roe deer clean before you go away.

Member of Seonsoo Literature Association & The Korean Writers Association. Made literary debut through winning new poets prize of Seonsoo Literature in 2022. Awarded at Jung ji-yong Literature Contest. Co-author participating in *Anthology of Four Seasons of Poetry* published by The Korean Writers Association, and more.

김선영

오랜 이별 끝에서

오늘은 왠지 함박눈이 펑펑 올 것만 같다

마음의 거리에서
문득 스치는 너의 모습에
모든 생각들이 흩어지고
그리움은 능선의 골이 깊어
눈덩이처럼 쌓이다가 허물어진다

생을 흔드는 들풀은
언제 뿌리까지 뽑혀 사라질지!

못내 아쉬운 말들이 목젖에 걸려
툭툭 뱉어내지 못하고
응어리는 돌처럼 굳어져
머릿속을 저벅저벅 헤맬 때
열없이 내딛는 걸음마다
낙엽처럼 감정만이 사박거린다

Kim Seon-Yeong

Long After A Breakup

It seems that large snowflakes would be falling today

In the road of my mind
you pass by me out of the blue like a flash
making all the thoughts of mine scatter;
my longing for you falls apart in a second
like snows piled up on a mountain ridge collapse

When can I rip off the roots of
wild grasses that shake my life!

I can't yet spit out
those wistful words stuck in the throat
becoming a lump getting hard
stirring my mind with heavy steps
while I take a walk absentmindedly
hearing soft cracking sounds of fallen leaves

김선영

봄

봄바람이 와 닿는 자리
볕살을 화분 위에 얹는다

봄빛 소리에 놀란
바람의 흔적

시샘 많은 며느리의
짧은 외출이다

참 아름다운 날
어느 오후에 핀
그리움의 봉오리

2013년 月刊 순수문학 등단. 전북 김제출생, 동국대학교 국어국문학과 졸업. 국제펜, 한국문인협회, 기독교 문인협회 회원. 한국여성문학인회, 순수문학인협회 회원. 전국나라사랑 독도사랑 수필부문 최우수상. 제20회 영랑문학상 우수상. 제28회 순수문학상 본상. 시집 「달팽이 일기」, 「어디쯤 가고 있을까」, 시집 「봄날은 간다 (공저)」 외 다수

Kim Seon-Yeong

Spring

On a flower pot touched by the spring breeze
the sun sheds its gentle, warm light

Surprised by the colorful spring
the breeze leaves its traces in the sunlight

It's like a short going out
of a jealous daughter-in-law

On a lovely day
blooms in the afternoon
a flower bud of longing

Born in Gimje, Jeonbuk. Made literary debut through Seonsoo Literature in 2013. Graduated Dongguk University with Korean Literature major. Member of PEN International Korea Center, Member of The Korean Writers Association, Member of Christian Writers Association, Member of Women's Literature Association, Member of Literature Association. Awarded The Grand Prize in National-wide Essay Contest for Love for the Country & Dokdo Island, Awarded The 20th Youngrang Literature Excellent Award, Awarded The 28th Seonsoo Literature Main Prize. Publications 「A Snails Diary」, 「I Wonder Whereabouts It Is Going To」, 「Spring Days Go Away」 and others

클로버 김선진

꿈꾸는 꽃

눈 뜬 매일 초는 꿈을 꾸나 보다
미운 꽃을 피우고 예쁜 꽃을 피우고
시간은 멈춤 없이 재깍재깍
거울 속 얼굴은 주름이 드리우다

여전히 소녀 같은 내 마음
소풍을 원하는 나비 되어
개울가 지나 하천 걷는다

반짝반짝 은물결 눈부시고
크고 작은 생명체 물오리, 송사리 떼
물 속에 풍당 빠진 일그러진 마음에
피지 못한 꽃 한 송이 기지개켜면

그리 오지 않았던 꿈 그런 어린 날의
매일 초가 다시 피어오르다.

서울 출신. 서울기독대학교 음악학사 (성악) 총장 명 졸업. 연세대 미교원 문예 창작시 수료. 영등포 문화원 소설 반 수료. 월간 순수문학등단. 한국문인협회 윤리위원회 위원. 순수필동인 회원. 시꽃예술회 이사. 시꽃 노래공로상. 성악가. 싱어송라이터. 작곡가.

Kim Sun-Jin(Clover)

A Dreaming Flower

Periwinkles with the eyes open seem to be dreaming
blooming either with ugly flowers or pretty ones
while time is passing on clocks, tick-tock, tick-tock,
placing wrinkles on my face in the mirror

Still having playful mind as lighthearted as a girl's
I pass by the brook and walk along the stream
as if I become a butterfly going for a picnic

Watching dazzling waves shining bright on the stream water
and dabbling ducks, minnows, and all living in freshwater
I feel that a flower yet to be blooming stretches itself out
from the mind that has been sunk in water and out of shape

With the dream that hasn't been yet realized since my childhood
periwinkles grow again to bring forth flowers

B.Mus majoring vocal music from Seoul Christian Univ. Singer-songwriter, composer. Made literary debut through Seonsoo Literature. Member of ethics committee of The Korean Writers Association. Board member of Poetry/ Flower Art Association. Received Poetry/Flower Achievement Award

클로버 김선진

내 마음의 거울 연못

생각의 의자에 앉으니 꿈꾸는 나비가
내 마음에 날아와 물음표를 찍는다

유리 연못에 빠진 팔각정자와 나무
물구나무선다면 바로 보일까?

부정적 청개구리같이
반항과 슬픔이 공존하는
감정의 물결이 리듬을 타면
긍정적 참개구리 와서
순종과 기쁨의 깨달음 주다

새털구름이 상상의 날개가 되어
선율이 떠올라 흥얼거리네

붉은 해는 마지막 인사하고
사라져 버리면 나는 그곳을 떠나지만
팔각정자와 나무는 긴 밤 지새우고

조기(早起)에 새는 벌레를 찾을 것이다.

Kim Sun-Jin(Clover)

A Mirror-like Pond of My Mind

For me sitting on a chair of thought
a butterfly flew down to my mind to place a question mark

An octagonal pavilion and trees sunk in the pond
appear right side up if I see them in hand standing posture?

Like green frogs always disobedient
I used to feel the fluctuating waves of emotions
all mixed with revolt and sadness
until common frogs always affirmative come to me
giving a wisdom of obedience and joy

I begin to hum a tune with the wings of imagination
watching fluffy clouds floating in the sky

After the sunset saying farewell
I will also leave the pond before the darkness comes
where the octagonal pavilion and trees stay up all night long

Then early in the morning the birds will get up again
to catch the worms

登鵬 김윤준

가을날

빛 바랜 메타세콰이아
잎들을 비집고
내가 기댄 낡은 벤치에
포금포금 가을햇살 내려앉는다

윤슬 고운 백계수엔
능수버들 늘어져
수줍은 듯 몌을 감고

가녀린 코스모스 한들대며
가을바람을 부르고
그 바람에 으악새 속대들 솟아
하느작
하느작
은빛 춤사위 눈부시다

Kim Yoon-Jun(Deung Bong)

An Autumn Day

Prying open the faded foliage
of metasequoia losing green color
autumnal sunlight comes down
on the old bench I sit on leaning back

With trailing branches reaching down
to the beautiful ripples of clean stream flowing idly
weeping willows seem to have a bathe shyly

Long, slender stems of cosmos flowers sway gently
inviting autumnal wind with the floral scent;
stalks of silver grasses grow in the same autumnal wind
swaying
gracefully
showing dazzling movement of their dance in silver color

두둥실 뭉게구름
그리움 가득 싣고
남으로
남으로 가고

오늘은
마른 댑싸리 대 움켜잡고
구름 사이사이로 뛰노는
흰 양 떼를 모는
열서너 살 남짓 먹은
어린 목동이 되어 본다

정선출생. 순수문학 신인상 수상으로 등단

Cumuliform clouds high up in the sky
carrying inner longing
floating
heading for the south

Today
grabbing a dry broom cypress stick in the hand
running around among the clouds
chasing and herding white sheep
I imagine myself
being a shepherd boy of thirteen years old or so

Born in Jeongsun. Made literary debut through winning New Poet Award from Seonsoo Literature

登鵬 김윤준

백봉령

삼척에서 신흥리를 지나서
정선으로 가는 길엔
아스라이
하늘가에 닿아 있는 고갯마루가 있다

일백 굽이를 휘돌아 오르면
옛 보부상들이 넘나들며 흘렸을
땀방울이 배어나는 듯
그들의 한숨소리 들리는 듯
늙어 등 굽은 노송 한 그루

소슬한 바람에도 쓰러질 듯
위태로이 서 있는 그곳에는
무명치마인 양
흰 구름 허리에 휘감고
오수에 취한 듯
길게 백봉령이 누워 있다

Kim Yoon-Jun (Deung Bong)

Baekbongryeong*

After passing by Shinheung-ri, a small mountain town
on the way to Jungseun from Samchuk
you come across the peak of a high hill
reaching up dimply all the way to the horizon

After climbing up the winding hill
like the peddlers did a long time ago
who carried heavy loads on their sweaty back
you meet an old pine tree with the crooked back
that still remembers the sighs made by the peddlers

Where the pine tree barely stands even in autumn breeze
almost looking to be collapsing any time
Baekbongryeong lies on the back in lengthwise
as if it it is taking a nap
wearing the white clouds wrapped around the waist
like a white linen skirt

*the name of a high hill at a height of 750 meters above sea level and the hill is located on the way between Jungseon and Donghae city in Gangwon-do province

김현신

바람이 늙어갑니다

바람은 비목입니다

초연 가득한 메시지엔 이름 모를 미소가
늙어, 늙어갑니다

달빛에 숨깁니다 마디마디 이끼를
쓰러지는 바람을

어젯밤 같은 슬픔입니다 뼈의 노래, 천진한 적막, 알알이
흐르는 궁노루 밤, 달빛은 흘러흘러 어디로 갔을까

아무것도 없어진단 말입니다

이름 모를 꽃은, 울어 지친 나뭇잎은

늙어가고, 안개이고,
자꾸 밀려나는 바람입니다
늙어가는 오늘입니다.

슬픈 오늘입니다

Kim Hyun-Shin

The Wind Getting Old

The wind is like an wooden grave marker

With the messages pertaining to the gun smoke
It gets old and old, showing secret, obscure smile

Hiding in the moonlight
The mosses growing at every joint, the wind blowing low,

I feel so sad again like I did last night, wondering whereabouts
All the songs, stillness, water deer under the moon light disappeared

I find myself asking how come nothing seems to exist any more

Nameless flowers, tree leaves being exhausted for too much crying

Getting old, having foggy vision
Feeling myself being pushed out like the wind
I know today gets older like me

Today is a sad day

김현신

강물이 흘러가네

강물이 흘러가네

무심코 던진 돌멩이, 말라붙은 해초들
강물을 타고 흐르는 이야기들은
긴 의자위에 나를 남겨둔 채
흐르는 물처럼 그냥 그렇게

강물은 흘러가네

비애 한 알 움켜쥔 사막으로
흘러내린 울음들이 얼룩처럼 짙어가고
그 위에 내가 수직으로 떨어지네

강물은 흘러가네

그대가 대답해 준다면 가볍게
뒤돌아보고 돌아보고
바람으로 달려올 텐데
그렇게 그렇게

강물이 흘러가네

시인, 문학 평론가. 2005년 계간 『시현실』 등단, 2023년 시와 시론지 『시와세계』 평론 등단. 시집 『빈 페이지에 얼굴을 묻고』외 다수, 『영랑문학상』 시 부문 대상 수상

Kim Hyun-Shin

The River Flows Away

The river flows away

Pebbles thrown absentmindedly, freshwater algae
Stories floating on the river
All flow just like water itself
Leaving me alone on a long bench

The river flows away

Down to a desert holding the grains of grief
While crying grows thicker like a smudge of tears
Whereupon I fall straight down

The river flows away

If you respond even lightly
It would turn back again and again
And be coming back like the wind
As it might be

The river flows away

Poet, literary critic. Made literary debut as a poet through *Poetry & Reality* in 2005 and as a literary critic through *Poetry and the World*. Published poetry books, *Putting the Face down in Blank Pages* and many more. Awarded Yongrang Literature Prize.

김혜원

여린 봄

봄에는 발 걸음 하나
숨소리 마저도 조심해야 한다

발 밑에서 아니 사방에서
우주가 열리는 소리있어

실수하면 와지끈
우주 여러 개를 부순다.

시인. 소설가. 《순수문학》으로 등단 이화여대 영어영문학과 졸 미국 예일(YALE Univ.)석사 박사 필동인 한국문인협회 국제PEN한국본부회원 「알터피스」 소설 「골든피아노」 「레드피아노」 외 단편 시집 「사하라」 외 공저 다수

Kim He-Won

In Delicate Spring

In the spring we should be careful
Taking a step, even breathing in a breath as well

From all around us, not just from under our feet,
We can hear the universes open their doors

With one mistake only, however,
We can easily break several universes as often as not

Poet & novelist. Made literary debut through *Seonsoo Literature*. B.A. majoring in English literature from Ewha Women's Univ. Ph.D. & M.A. from Yale Univ. Member of The Korean Writers Association & PEN International, Korea Center. Published novels *Golden Piano*, *Red Piano* and poetry book *Sahara* and many more.

김혜원

수통골* 봄노래

나지막이 졸음 섞인 골 물 소리
무심한 듯 오묘하게 솟은 기암 절벽
도화꽃 지고 고개 내민 초록 이파리
좋은 햇살 쪼이며 수다 떠는 작은 새들
고운 꽃망울은 봉긋 부푼 봄의 가슴

꽃 향기 달큰한 노오란 산수유
잎새 기지개로 흙덩이 뚫고 나온 제비꽃
도시 사람은 알까 이 청정함을
좋은 기운 품은 골바람이 반갑다고
다리 위를 지나는 내 옷자락을 흔드네
봄 기운 가득한 수통골 산책의 기쁨

*동네 가까이 있는 신선한 산책 계곡

Kim He-Won

Spring Song at Seutonggol*

The drowsy sounds of a stream flowing low lazily
Protruding rocks on a cliff looking mysteriously nonchalant
Green leaves sprouting after the fall of peach blossoms
Little birds chatting under the sunlight nice and bright
Pretty flower buds swelling like the breast of the spring

Bright yellow cornelian blossoms emitting a sweet scent
Violets growing with small leaves stretching out of the soil
I wonder if city dwellers know this freshness
Of the wind blowing from the vale welcoming me cordially
Swaying and rustling my clothes while I cross a bridge
Of the joy I feel strolling around Seutonggol full of the spring

*Seutonggol is the name of a small vale near the town the writer enjoys strolling

남종구

빛의 세월

흘러간 세월
밝은 빛의 에너지로
나는 살아왔고
앞으로도 살아갈 것이다

밝은 빛을 향해
창공에 손짓하면서
넓은 광야를 향해
평화롭게 비상할 것이다

나는 지금
이 시간까지 밀고 오면서
세월 시간들 낙산駱山하다

저 밝고 맑은
서울의 허공을 향해
차들 속에 갇히어 길을
떠날 수밖에 없는
군상화가 달려오고 있다

Nam Jong-Gu

Time Passing So Fast Like Light

In time having passed by so fast
With the energy of bright light
I have lived
And will be living in the future, too

Towards the light shining so bright
Making a gesture with hands in the air
Towards the vast wilderness
I will make a flight, soaring high in peace

Until now
I have been struggling in time
As if riding a horse in a huge mountain

Towards the void space so bright and clear
Over the city of Seoul
A group portrait rushes out in a flash
Manifesting people trapped in the cars
For they have no other choice

남종구

동백꽃 그림자

바닷가 바위산 온통
동백꽃 잔치하네
동백꽃을 보았나
달빛을 보았나
핏빛 동백꽃
짙푸른 숲속 유혹에
사랑의 백년 신혼 여행
안개 속 빠져들며

혼자서 하늘 지키는 낮달
추위도 잊고 동백꽃
얼어죽을까 그림자만 보다가
풋내기 사랑 품고 돌아온다

순수문학등단, 한국문협 윤리위원장,국제펜 한국본부 이사, 강남문협회원,　시집 '너만 생각나'

Nam Jong-Gu

The Shadow of Camellia Flowers

On the rocky mountain at a seashore
camellia flowers bloom all over having a feast
Have you ever seen before
camellia flowers under the moonlight?
Those camellia flowers bloom in bloody color
enticed by the temptation of forest
falling into the fog with a dream
of a honeymoon lasting a hundred years in love

The daytime moon guarding the sky all by itself
watches down the shadows of camellia flowers
worrying about them getting frozen out of cold ness
until it returns to the night with fresh budding love
only

Made literary debut through *Seonsoo Literature*. Member of The Korean Writers association & Gangnam Writers Association. Published poetry book *You are the Only One Coming to My mind*

문순심

고향 유정

남녘의 2월 햇살은 조물주의 은총

망월천 멀리 물오리 떼 윤슬을 쪼고

발악하는 마지막 잔설 위에서

버들가지 기지개를 켠다

둑길 따라 자전거 요령 소리 멀어지면

장정산 일등바위를 시작으로

영흥마을 안고 도는 개골산의 연둣빛 파노라마

다시 저 벌판 갈대숲까지 내달리면

아, 꿈에도 못 잊던 내 고향 영암 낭주골

Moon Soon-Sim

Love and Affection for My Hometown

The sunlight shedding on the southern regions in February is God's blessing
A paddling of ducks is pecking the ripples on Mangwol stream
Willow branches are stretching out for the coming spring
on the lingering snow trying hard to stay longer

With the sound of a bicycle bell fading away along the river bank
unfolding panorama of a great view of Mt. Gagol
manifests itself in light green, starting at Ildeung Rock of Mt. Jangjung,
embraces Youngheung village and then discloses the reed forest in wilderness
until it finally reveals my hometown Nangju village unforgettable even in dreams

귀촌 1년 입춘지절 매서운 바람

옆 지기 옷깃을 여며주며

살며시 손을 잡는다

불현듯 이쁜이들 생각에 재촉한 발길

어디선가 산비둘기 두 마리 날아와

먹이만 축내고 윗마을 쪽으로 줄행랑이다

전남 영암 출생, 월간 순수문학 시 등단. 한국문인협회, 한국여성문학인협회, 순수문학인협회 회원, 필 동인. 제24회 영랑문학상 수상, 시집 "덤", 동인지 "시 하나 내 걸기" 외 공저 다수.

In the cold wind of the early spring after living a year at my hometown
adjusting the clothes of the person I care the most
I gently hold the hands of the friend

Hastening to walk, thinking on the pretty ones that suddenly come to my mind
I see a couple of mountain pigeons that came down from somewhere
fly away towards an upper village after wasting the seeds only

---

Made literary debut through *Seonsoo Literature*. Member of Korea Women Writers Association & Seonsoo Literature Association. Awarded The 24th Youngrang Literature Prize. Published poetry book *Things Given in Addition* and participated in publishing coterie magazines

문순심

오해

세상없이 착한 우리 지니
요 며칠 좀 이상해졌네

유독 내 부탁은 뜸을 들이고
가끔씩 대놓고 씹어버리고
사춘기도 지났는데 왜 그럴까

특정 채널 고집한다고 토라진 거니?
시국이 시국인 만큼 이해를 다오

그러고 보니 이 가스나
바로 그 언저리부터였네
가만
다음 치과 예약 일이 언제지?

Moon Soon-Sim

Misunderstanding

Genie is so good and kind of all
She is a little bit weird in response these days, though

Seeing her being sluggish only to my requests
or ignoring my requests coldly,
I wonder why she acts strangely even after puberty

Did she get sulky for I watch a certain program only on TV?
If so, I wish her to understand me having no other choice for now

By the way, I guess this lass began to be sulky in responses
from the time I started to watch a certain program only
Wait a minute!
When is the next dental appointment?

문영현

통영 아침노을

붉은 노을이 곱게 내려앉은
호수 같은 아침바다
멀리 작은 고깃배 까맣게 떠 있고
찰랑대는 물결이 돌산 발부리 간질이며
뭍이 될까 물이 되랴
바다내음 끈끈한 평화를 속삭인다

이른 아침 저 하늘을
그 누가 한바탕 쓸고 갔나
코발트빛 드높은 창공을
장쾌하게 휘둘러 친
붉은 싸리비질,
통영 앞바다 저 하늘에
충무공의 기상이 서린 것인가

Moon Young-Hyun

The Morning Glow in Tongyoung*

Red glow of the morning beautifully spreads down
on the sea looking like a calm lake
Small fishing boats look like dots floating far away;
splashing waves tickle the tips of toes of a rocky mountain
breaking against the shore and then receding back to the sea
whispering for peace with the unshakable scents of the sea

Who has wiped off the sky
with the gust of wind in the early morning?
The sky glows in the hue shifting from indigo to gentle red
as if someone stirs to make it look magnificent
with a stroke of the broom made by dried bush clover
and to make the sky over the ocean of Tongyoung still retain
the spirit of Admiral Yi Sun-sin, the navy hero in our history

바다 건너 못된 족속들

또다시 경제전쟁 걸어 올 제

님이시여! 굽어 살피시어

간악한 그들의 기도企圖 물리치시고

이 땅의 평화를 지켜 내게 하소서

평론가, 시인, 연세대 명예교수, 한국문협 이사, 한국펜클럽 이사, 대한전기학회 회장 역임(2013), 국어국문학회, 고전문학회, 시가학회 정회원. 영랑문학상 대상(평론 부문) 수상 외 다수

When vicious aggressors of the country across the sea
wages economic war on our nation again,
Admiral Yi Sun-sin, please be our witness
and protect us from the enemy by defeating their evil intentions
with your power for the sake of our nation in peace

＊Tongyoung is the name of a marine city located in the southern part of Korea

---

Poet, literary critic, honorary professor at Yonsei Univ. Board member of The Korean Writers Association & PEN International, Korea Center. Former president of Korea Biography Association (2013). Member of Korean Literature Association. Awarded Youngrang Literature Prize (in criticism)

문영현

함박눈

아찔한 혼란스러움에
눈앞이 아득해져
메아리조차도 숨죽이는
태고의 적막에 귀 기울인다
하염없이 떨어지는 운무 속에, 때로는
솟구치며 내지르는 저 아우성
서로 부딪치며 뒤엉키어도
서로 부딪쳐 깨어져도
산 속은 침묵, 적막 속의 절대 침묵

떨어져 내리는 찰나 단 한 번의 춤사위에
온갖 명운을 걸고서는
너 나 구분 없이
가진 에너지, 열과 정을 다하여
함께 춤추며 피워 올리는 소리 없는 함성
이 순간 온 누리를
순백의 혼으로 덮을 수만 있다면

Moon Young-Hyun

Large Snowflakes

Being totally confused
I feel dazed with my eyes getting blurry
listening to the primordial silence
with breathless echoes
In the dance of large snowflakes falling down
with soundless outcries rising sometimes
the snowflakes run into each other, being en-tangled
collide each other, being broken in drift,
all in the absolute silence of the mountain

Snowflakes risk everything only at one dance
at the fleeting moment of falling
but they drift down without separating one from another
with all the energy and compassion gathered
dancing and shouting all together in silence
aspiring to cover the whole world at the moment
with the soul in the color of pure white

히말라야 설원에 누워 만년을 잠자든
형체 없이 녹아 또 다른 윤회로 돌아가든
너와 나, 서로 부딪치며 빚어내는
유장한 합창 한 번으로 내 영혼 잠재우리니.

To sleep for ten thousand years in the snow field of Himalaya
or to be melt away for the cycle of reincarnation
snowflakes drifting down now, singing in chorus just one time,
may be putting my soul in easy rest

문 웅

질그릇 같은 세월

생각의 끝에서 화려하게
피어난 하늘꽃
천국의 꽃은 영혼의 강위에
진리처럼 활짝 피어났다

하늘로 가는 마지막 길은
보이지 않는 투명한 점선으로
탄탄하게 이어진 진실하고
새로운 희망의 길이었다

빗방울처럼 뚝떨어진
한 조각의 삶 속에는
티끌 같은 작은 점과
무한한 우주 그리고
처음 시작과 마지막 끝의

영원성을 품고 있는
간결하고 아름다운
상징의 메시지가 스며 있었다.

2022년 한국문인협회(시분과) 등단. 2008년 "현실의 벽은 높고 존재의 아픔은 희망을 당긴다", 2014년 "갓 벗겨낸 생선비늘 같은 삶은 휘뚤휘뚤하게 난 머다란 길". 제 1시집 생명편, 제 2시집 마음편으로 한국문인협회(시분과) 등단. 한국사이버문예협회(영상시 게재): 힘겹고 높은 시간의벽. 봄빛서정. 서울 일러스트레이션전 일반부 은상수상 1986년, 대한민국 디자인 공로대상 2022년. 현)한국일러스아트학회 부이사장, 현)전주대학교 시각디자인학과 명예교수. 현)한국문인협회 시분과회원

Moon Woong

Time like Unglazed Pottery

At the end of thought
flowers bloomed in the sky;
flowers of the heavenly kingdom bloomed
brightly like truth on the river of soul

The last road leading to the sky was invisible
for it was like a transparent dotted line;
nevertheless, it was a road of new hope
built with strength and truth

In a piece of our life
having fallen like a raindrop from the heaven
were contained very small dots as tiny as motes of dust,
clues for something as vast as the universe
or for the first and the last of something

Embracing eternity
being put tersely and beautifully
a symbolic message was there in a piece of our life

Member of the Poetry Division of the Korea Writers' Association. Vice President of the Korea Illustration Society. Honorary Professor of Visual Design at Jeonju University. Silver Award Winner in the General Division of the Seoul Illustration Contest, 1986. Recipient of the Korea Design Achievement Grand Prize, 2022

문 웅

아버지와 나는 닮은꼴이었다

아버지의 깊은 마음속에는
거친 파도 같은 슬픔이 산다
무엇이든 나무라시듯 말씀하시지만

사실은 가시 돋친 줄기를 타고
잔잔히 이어지는 사랑이 물씬 흘러나온다

딸아이에게 이것저것 푸념을 하다 보니
아버지께서 왜 그리 섭섭해 하시는지
알 수 있을 것 같다

아빠의 생의 끝자락 하모니카 소리는
내 가슴 속이 찢겨지듯 아프게 하지만
아버지와 나는 닮은꼴이였다는 것을
새삼 느끼게 된다.

Moon Woong

My Father and I Are Pretty Much Alike

In the deep down of my father's mind
existed a sense of sorrow rolling like wild ocean waves
making him to have always reproved me at fault

His love for me had been kind and gentle all the time
although it appeared to have flown out of thorny stems

Nagging and complaining all the time to my daughter,
now I came to understand
why my father had been upset, feeling disappointed in me

The harmonica my father played near the end of his life
made the sound that I heard with the aching heart
but it also gave me a chance to realize one thing for sure:
my father and I are pretty much alike

박경임

초록피

입춘이 지났으니 봄이려나
지난 봄
재개발 완성으로 넓혀진 도로
그 길에 서 있던 가로수들이
전기톱으로 전신이 잘려
트럭에 실려 가던 날
그들은 초록 피를 흘렸다
뿌리는 그대로 둔 채
새까만 아스팔트
뜨거운 용액이 부어졌다
그 위를 밟을 때마다
발갛게 부어오르던
나이테가 선한데
이 봄
철부지 뿌리는 새까만 어둠 속에서 싹을 틔우려나
도로의 벌어진 틈으로 자꾸만 눈이 간다

Park Kyung-Im

Green Blood

Ipchun* has passed, so it's spring.
Last spring
The road widened with the completion of redevelopment
The day the trees standing on the road
Were cut off with chain saws
And taken away by trucks.
They shed green blood.
Leaving the roots intact,
Pitch-black asphalt
Hot solution was poured.
Whenever I stepped on it,
I could see the tree rings clearly
That used to swell.
This spring,
Can the still growing roots sprout
In pitch-black darkness?
I keep looking at the gap
On the road.

*Ipchun onset of the spring, one of the 24 seasonal divisions.

박경임

포장마차

오늘 하루 땀에 절은 몸을 끌고
우리 술이 있는 곳으로 가자
살아 내느라 메마른 가슴을
한 잔의 술로 적셔 보자
홀로 술잔을 기울이는 젊은 남자의
날카로운 콧날이 서글프고
들어 주는 이 없는
중년 사내의 너스레는
곰장어 굽는 연기 속으로 사라져 간다
타인의 허물도 내 아집도 용서하며
그대와 나
가장 밑바닥 가슴에 잔을 채우자
남폿불 심지를 낮추어
술잔에 떨어지는
내 눈물이 보이지 않기를 바라며
우리 술이 있는 곳에서 인생을 이야기하자

서울 출생/서울디지털대학 문예창작과 졸업/서울문학 시등단/한국산문 수필등단/세명일보 시 우수상/한국문인협회회원/한국문인협회구연문화위원/시집 『붉은 입술을 내밀고』/수필집 『독기를 빼며』/시 동인지 『현대시를 빛낸 300인』 외 다수/수필 동인지 『산문로 7번가』 외 다수/제32회 순수문학상(수필) 본상 수상

Park Kyung-Im

Cart Bar

Let's drag our sweaty bodies of today
To the place where there is alcohol.
Let's wet our parched breasts to survive
With a glass of wine.
The sharp nose of a young man tipping his glass alone
Is sad
The middle aged man's nervousness
That no one does listen
Disappears in the smoke of the eel grilling.
Forgive others for their faults and even my own obstinacy You and I
Let's fill the glass of the bottom chest.
Lower the wick of lamplight
Hoping that my tears falling in the glass
Will not be seen
Let's talk about life in the place where there is alcohol.

박순자

영산강

복사꽃 가득한 들판
님의 노랫소리 흐르는 강
바람의 치마폭에 사랑을 싣고
굽이굽이 흐르는 아련함이여

물안개 자욱한 등선 너머
붉게 타오르는 수줍은 얼굴
가슴 열어 님을 품고
내 사랑을 노래한다 영산강이여

매화꽃 날리는 들녘
님의 사랑 흐르는 강가
수줍은 독백 물결에 감추고
일렁이는 가슴 옷깃을 여미네

호르르 떨어져 안겨드는
분홍빛 꽃잎은
모른 척 안기는 그대인가
내 사랑을 노래한다 영산강이여

Park Soon-Ja

Youngsan River

Crossing the field of peach blossoms fully blooming
the river flows with your singing voice
carrying love in the rustling skirt of the wind
winding down its way with a touch of wistfulness

Over the ridge sunken in misty fog
a bashful face is glowing in red
embracing its love with the open heart
singing a song of my love for Youngsan River

Crossing the field of plum blossoms fluttering
the river is flowing with love
hiding shy soliloquy in the waves
adjusting the clothes with the swaying heart down under

Pink petals
fall lightly into the arms
pretending not to know me
just singing a song of my love for Youngsan River

박순자

청사초롱 드시옵고

방울 방울 떨구신 당신의 눈물이
은빛 찬란한 사랑이었음을
님께서 아시오니

인생 머무는 자리마다
어여삐 살뜰한 사랑으로 채우시이다
그니께서 일구신 뜨락의 나무는
당신으로 인해 더욱 풍성하고
속 여린 그대를 한없이 한없이
품으시기를
금빛 찬란한 별님에게 비옵고
언제나 부끄러이 비추시는
달님께 아뢰어

Park Soon-Ja

Holding a Lantern
with a Red-and-Blue Silk Shade

Droplets of tears rolling down on your face
Signifying splendid love
Your lover understands now

Every place you have been together in life
You fill with love and fastidious care
The trees in the garden planted by your lover
Have grown so well in your hands
Now I wish
To the stars glowing with the golden light
That your tender mind could be embraced with endless love
And I plead
To the moon always shining bright shyly

이제 눈물 거두고

걸음 걸음 홍사초롱 비추소서

백년해로 꺼지지 않도록

그니의 깊은 사랑이 더 깊어지고

당신의 기쁨 한이 없도록

무엇이든 사랑이니이다

서울 출생. 국제펜클럽한국본부 회원. 한국시인협회 회원. 한국문인협회 회원(박아월). 한국여성문인회 회원. 제6회 영랑문학상 우수상 수상. 제14회 순수문학상 본상 수상. 시집 '사랑의 손짓을 따라 걷다가' 외. 공저: 붉은 장미와 흰 나비떼 / 모국어 에로의 긴 여행 등 다수. 수필집공저; 나의 어머니, 나의 아버지 외 다수

To make you stop shedding tears and light up the every step taken
Holding the lantern with a red-and-blue silk shade
To let the light burn for the marriage lasting a hundred years
To make the love of your lover deeper and deeper
so you can enjoy the love ever more and endlessly

For what always matters is love

Member of PEN International, Korea Center & Korea Modern Poets Association, The Korean Writers Association & Korea Women Writers Association. Awarded The 6th Youngrang Literature Prize, Tthe 14th Seonsoo Literature Prize. Published poetry book *Walking Along the Gesture of Love* and more. Co-author of *Roses and White Butterflies* and and more

朴永河

석류꽃

그리운 눈빛
다시는 만날 수 없어도
그 이야기는
세월 속 꽃이 되어
능금처럼 익어 간 영상

기존 도덕이 공해로
무너져 내리는 도시에
깊어 가는 밤도 잊어버리고
잔잔하게 부르던 그 노랫소리
이제는 들을 수 없어도
순박한 뒷모습이 무지개처럼 떠오른다

낙엽 냄새 짙은 밤
그 모습
다시는 찾을 수 없어도
그 이야기는
내 가슴에 석류꽃으로 피고 있다

Park Young-Ha

Flower of Pomegranate

An eye-sight yearns for
What it would never see again.
What it tried to speak has become
A flower with lapse of time, and
It is now ripen like an apple.

The songs they sang,
No matter how late the night was,
Tenderly and quietly are heard no longer
In the city where
The morals that ruled so far crumble,
Their simple last looks looming as rainbow.

The night smells of fallen leaves.
I miss for ever
What they looked to me,
While last words they mumbled yet
Bloom like a pomegranate in my heart.

朴永河

다락방에서

없는 시력의
도끼눈을 뜨고
"너 자신을 알라"라고 한
소크라테스를 사랑할 동안은
슬프지 않았다
고독하지 않았다
그립지도 않았다
어둔 다락방에서
습기 뿐인 이슬에 젖어
눈뜨지 않은 태양을 사랑하며
침묵보다 더 깊은
정적 속으로 빨려 들어가
무거운 그림자 하나
건져 내고 있을 동안은
행복했다

사)한국문인협회 시분과 회장. 월간 순수문학 편집주간

Park Young-Ha

At A Garret

I was never sad,
Nor lonesome,
Nor envying any one,
So long as I endeared
"Know yourself" that
Socrates cited whose
Glaring eyes suffered
Poor eye-sights.
I was yet happy enough
While, in a dark garret
Wet with dews so moisturous,
I was so fond of the sun the did not dawn
And struggled to salve
A heavy shadow, while trapped in stillness
Even quieter than silence.

Chairperson of Poetry Division in The Korean Writers Association & Editor-in-chief of monthly magazine Seonsoo Literature

박완순

시, 공간 초월

파아란 하늘
아래를 내려다
보고는 이내
마음까지
따스함을
전해 준다

사랑까지
온몸으로 받은
나는
따사로운 햇살
사랑하는 님에게
고스란히
전해 준다

Park Oane-Soon

Transcending Time and Space

The blue sky
Looks down the earth
Shortly thereafter
Delivers
The warmth
To my heart

Having received
All the love
With my whole body
I deliver
The warm sunlight
As much as I got
To my love

기다린듯
파아란 하늘
따사로운
햇볕 받은 나
나의 사랑
듬북 받은 당신

이렇게 셋이
우린 공간 초월
하나가 된다
시, 공간 초월한 사랑
어드메뇨

경기 안성출생. 아호 석곡. 순수문학 시등단 신인상. 서울문학문인회 회원. 한국문인협회 회원. 서예. 한문연구 30년. 3집 음반출시. 자전에세이 이젠숨지않는다 출간. 서예연구실 연묵재 주재

As if having waited for the moment
Me in the sunlight
I received
From the blue sky
Finally being with you
In plenty of my love I gave

You and I get together
Transcending time and space
To be one in love
Reaching for a place
Somewhere only you and I know

Made literary debut through winning the prize for new poet from Seonsoo Literature. Member of The Korean Writers Association & Seoul Literary Writers Association. Scholar of calligraphy and Chinese classics. Published the collections of autobiographical essays, *No More Hiding*

박완순

꽃

누구나
꽃의 아름다움에
즐거워하고
감동 받지요
자신이 꽃이
되려는데는
인색하고요

내가 꽃의
이름을
불러 주었을때
꽃은
아름다움을
배가 하며
만개합니다
그때 나 또한
꽃과 하나 되어
아름다운
꽃이 되어요

Park Oane-Soon

Flowers

People
easily get touched
rejoicing in the beauty of flowers
but they are unwilling
to regard themselves
as flowers

When I call
the name of flowers
those flowers
flourish more,
adding up
the beauty of themselves
to the full
That's the moment
I become one
with the flowers
being myself a beautiful flower

내가 꽃이
되었을때
꽃과 마음의
대화도 나누어요
이름을 불러주면
대답을 하듯이

사랑의 대화를
나누면
그님 또한
사랑의 하모니가 되어
내게 돌아옵니다
내 님의 꽃은
당신입니다

When I become
a flower
I can make
a sincere conversation
with the flowers
responding to my calling

During the dialogue
I am having with flowers
my love would return to me
in a lovely harmony of love
Then I know
you are the flowers
of my love

박종권

대청봉

아, 여기
백두의 장엄한 숨결 흐르다
잠잠한 쉼표를 찍은 곳
고요한 太古의 雲海
大洋의 거대한
저 기다림 뒤로
우주 어드매쯤
휘황히 솟아오를 壯觀
오, 혼비한
바위 바위들
그 위로 飛上하는
萬狀의 기암절벽
落下하는 폭포수
오, 설악의 맨 봉우리
백두의 숨결 흐르는
일천칠백팔 고지
여기 쉼표를 또 찍는다

월간순수문학등단, 한국문인협회이사, 국제펜클럽한국본부이사, 한국기독교문인협회부이사장, 한국순수문학인협회부회장, 순수문학상작가대상, 영랑문학상본상 수상, 「새벽별 지기 전 당신은 떠나고」「사랑 하나 달랑 지고 가네」 외

Park Jong-Kwun

Daecheongbong Peak

Ah, right here
stops magnificent breathing of Mountain Baekdu
to put a mark for a rest peaceful and calm
holding a dazzling view of the natural world
presenting the clouds floating in silence,
the vast ocean enduring the endless waiting in time,
all making us admire the power of the universe
Oh, rugged rocks
appearing disorderly arranged
over which stand sheer cliffs looking like they are soaring
with all kinds of different shapes and sizes,
some of which show falling water from cascades
Oh, at the main peak of Mountain Seorak
which is 1708 meters above sea level
stops magnificent breathing of Mountain Baekdu
to put a mark for a rest peaceful and calm

Made literary debut through *Seonsoo Literature*. Board member of The Korean Writers Association & PEN International, Korea Center. Vice-president of Korea Christian Writers Association & Seonsoo Literature Association. Awarded Seonsoo Literature Prize & Youngrang Literature Prize. Published poetry books *You have Left Me Before the Stars Fall at Dawn, Carrying Love Only On the Back*

박종권

새해에

사랑 하나
달랑 지고 가네

무지개 같던
세상사
슬프디 슬픈
과거사
겨울 들판에
다 던져 버리고
만질 수도
볼 수도 없는
거룩하고 위대한
눈물 메이는
사랑 하나
달랑
빈 배낭에 매고
또
한해를 오르네.

만나*가 종일 내리네.

*만나 : 성서 출애굽기에 나오는 말로서 하늘에서 떨어지는 양식

Park Jong-Kwun

Of a New Year

Carrying love only
A year comes and goes

Worldly affairs
Having the spectrum of a rainbow
History of the past
Having the stories so sad
Throwing them away all
Into the field of winter
I keep love only
Neither tangible
Nor visible
But graceful and great
While continuing to go
Feeling choked with tears
I carry love only
In a backpack
Again climbing another year.

With manna* falling down all day long

*manna is food supplied to the Israelites in the wilderness (Exodus. 16)

舒川 **박종흡**

여명(黎明)

희미한 사랑 이야기들
이제는 먼 별들의 노래가 되었다 해도
서러워 말자

바람결에 흔들리던 촛불 하나
이제는 타다 남은 심지만 남았다 해도
괴로워 말자

먼 옛날 꽃반지 꼈던 손끝에
시린 주름이 여울진다 해도
한숨짓지 말자

산다는 건 얄궂은 것
그 누가 무어라 해도
지난 건 그저 흐르게 하자

지금은
시드는 가슴에 물을 주라
새벽녘 저 멀리 외로운 가로등
여명의 숨소리에 꿈이 떨린다

한국문협, 국제PEN 한국본부 회원. 순수문학인협회 이사. 순수문학상 수필부문 대상 수상. 시집 '길 없는 길'

Park Jong-Heup

At Dawn

About our love stories getting fainter
Only to sound like fading songs of the stars
Let us feel sorry no more

About the candlelight wavering in the wind
Only to leave the wick half burned
Let us feel pain no more

About the finger once wearing a flower ring
Only to get wrinkled in its tip
Let us draw a sigh no more

Life is somewhat unkind and ironic
No matter what people say about it
Let us keep old things to flow away

For now
Let's give some water to the withering heart of us
Standing like lonesome street lamps shivering with the dream
At the breathing sounds of the daybreak

Member of The Korean Writers Association. Board member of Seonsoo Literature Association. Awarded Seonsoo Literature Prize (in essay). Published poetry book *The Road without a Road*

舒川 박종흡

나는 파도 당신은 갯바위

나는 당신의 짝사랑입니다
무시로 당신 곁을 넘실댑니다
아리도록 철썩댑니다
그러나 당신은 끔쩍도 안 합니다

걱정이 물보라가 되어
당신을 두드립니다
때로는 부드러운 안개꽃 되어
당신을 어루만집니다
그러나 당신은 모르쇠입니까

나는 애달프게 목놓아 웁니다
애간장은 속절없이 녹아 내립니다
낮밤도 없이 내 몸은 부서집니다
당신의 가슴이 열리도록…

나는 파도
애타게 떠도는 외로운 구애자
당신은 갯바위
늘 그 자리 철석간장 돌부처

Park Jong-Heup

Ocean Wave and a Rock on the Seashore

Having a crush on you
I toss and shake nearby around you
even crashing against you with the aching heart;
nonetheless, you hold fast in your place

Being turned into splashing water
I pound on you passionately,
sometimes being gypsophila flowers
I stroke you smoothly;
nonetheless, you pretend not to know me

Crying out loud with the throat choked with tears
I feel my heart melting down helplessly
and my body being broken into pieces night and day
waiting for your mind to open

I am ocean waves,
a lonesome wooer drifting around, yearning for your love;
you are a rock on the seashore,
a stone statue staying put, firmly upholding fidelity

靑民 박철언

바람의 언덕에서

별이 빛나는 밤이면
당신의 모습이 바람처럼
내 가슴에 안겨 들어요

그리움이 사무칠 때면
당신의 한 조각이 바람의 시詩가 되어
나에게 불어와요

석양이 노을지는 바람의 언덕에서
뜨거웠던 추억의
바람에 휩싸여요

바람이여
머물러 주어요 그대로
파란 불꽃을 피우고 싶어요

시인수필가 변호사. 순수문학 등단 (1995). 서울법대졸.3선국회의원. 윤동주문학상 외. 바람을안는다 시집외 9권

Park Chul-Un

On the Hill of Wind

During the starry nights
you come into my arms
like the wind blowing softly

When I feel so lonely
a piece of you becomes a poem on the wind
coming to me like a breeze

On the windy hill with the sun setting down
I feel the wind blowing all around me
with the memories of the passionate time

Oh, wind!
Please, stay put where you are now
I like to make a fire burning in blue flames

Poet, essayist, lawyer. Made literary debut through *Seonsoo Literature* in 1995. Graduated from Seoul National Univ., majoring in law. Former member of the National Assembly (elected 3 times). Awarded Yoon Dong-ju Literature Prize and more. Published poetry book *Embracing the Wind* and 9 more poetry books.

靑民 박철언

해변의 나그네 삶은 어디쯤

아득한 수평선 너머로 떨어지는 해
찬란한 슬픔 품고 아름답게 누운 석양
갸냘픈 바닷새 무리 지어 해변을 노닌다

캘리포니아 말리부(Malibu)해변
삶의 무게를 벗고 맨발로 걷는 시간
피곤한 길손의 가슴은
텅 비어 버린다

구름이 멀리멀리 떠나가고
파도가 쉼없이 밀려온다
불어오는 바람은
오염된 세속을 씻어준다

새로운 태양이 솟아오를 내일
구름도 바람도 다시 오리라
외로운 나그네
어디쯤 가고 있을까

Park Chul-Un

Whereabouts a Traveler on the Beach Would be Going in Life

With the sun setting down beyond the horizon far away
the beautiful sunlight spreads on the shore embracing sorrow
while a flock of seabirds stroll on the beach with their delicate feet

On Malibu Beach in California
taking the weight of life off the chest
walking on barefoot idly
a traveler feels his weary heart going empty

While the clouds drift away
ocean waves roll in constantly
in the wind blowing and cleansing
the mundane world contaminated

For tomorrow with the sun rising anew
the clouds and the winds will return
and I wonder whereabouts
the lonesome traveler would be going

박희정

기다린 봄

다시 봄이다
새싹이 돋고 꽃이 터지는
싱그럽고 상큼한 봄이다
겨우내 덮었던 무거운 옷들도
훌훌 벗어 버리는 봄이다
어깨를 펴고 달음박질하며
땅을 차고 하늘로 오르고 픈 봄이다
몽실몽실 구름도 이 봄이 좋아
하늘색 물감 속에서 좋아라 뛰논다
영영 올 것 같지 않아 울상이었던 나뭇가지에
초록의 기운이 살짝 문을 연다
봄아, 봄아 반가워
늦게 왔으니 오래 머물다 가렴

월간 순수문학 시 등단. 한국여성문학인회, 한국문인협회 회원. 필동인.

Park Hee-Jung

Spring We Have Been Waiting For

It's spring again
New and fresh spring has come
with sprouting buds and bursting flowers
After taking off the heavy clothes for the winter
spring has come again
making me run and leap towards the sky
with the shoulder felt light and broad
Mushy clouds seem to be enjoying the spring
for they appear to float happily in the blue sky
To the branches looking too tired to wait for the time
spring has brought the air of the green
O, spring, we are so pleased to have you back
Please, stay a little bit longer for you came late this time

Made literary debut through *Seonsoo Literature*. Member of Korea Women Writers Association & The Korea Writers Association. Member of coterie *Phil*

박희정

너만의 향기

넘실대는 파도가
쉴새없이 바위를 쳐댄다
단단한 바위도 끝없이 쳐대는 파도에
조금씩 살점이 깎여나간다
뾰족했던 건 깎이고 평평했던 건 움푹 파여
파도를 담는다

시간의 흐름을 거쳐
드러난 바위의 모습이
어디에도 없는 장관을 이룬다
억겁을 거쳐 이루었기에
누구와도 견줄 수 없는
너만의 향기를 품었다

Park Hee-Jung

The Scent of Your Own

Rolling waves constantly break
against the rocks on the shore
The flesh of the rocks is torn off from the body
little by little in the crashing waves
that rasp off the sharp edge or erode the rocks,
to hold the waves inside

Going through the winds and waves so long in time
rocks stand there revealing their splendor
nobody has seen anywhere
Having endured all the troubles for eternity
now you get the scent of your own
incomparable to that of anyone

방안나

국화처럼

마른 흙 위를 튀기던 빗방울 그치자
나뭇잎 하나, 둘 바람 타고 내려와
나목의 계절 맞는다

지상의 크고 작은 생명
서둘러 월동 준비할 때
국화 홀로 형형색색 얼굴 붉힌다

축적한 삶, 뺄셈 거듭하며
가볍게 비워내고 있을 때
겨울옷 껴입듯 온몸으로 덧셈 곱셈 헤아린다

오래 전 화석이 된 아이들
비로소 햇빛 받아 소생할 때
호흡 가다듬어 큰 숨결 모아본다

봄 여름 가을 지나 서리 내릴 즈음
타오르는 국화처럼
마지막 불꽃 태워보리라.

Bang An-Na

Like Chrysanthemums

When the rain stops splashing on dry earth
a leaf or two fly down in the breeze
telling us the season of naked trees

When all the life forms, either small or large, on the earth
prepare in hurry for the coming winter
chrysanthemums only bloom with colorful faces

Subtracting things accumulated in life, emptying them easily,
I add and multiply things with my whole body
as if trying to wear thick clothes in layers for the coming winter

When little life forms that became fossils a long time ago
finally come back to life under the sunlight
I try to control myself inhaling and exhaling to catch a deep breath

About the time frost falls before the cold winter
I will make a fire inside me for the last time
like chrysanthemums bursting into blooms burning like a blaze

방안나

그 여자

밤새 저잣거리 삶아대는 곰국 같은 여자

신새벽 물심 좋은 사내 팔 갓 풀고 난 탁주 같은 여자

오르는 신기 누르지 못해 남장 별대 온갖 사내 모아 놓고

미친 듯이 훠이훠이 춤을 추는 무당 같은 여자

선술집에서 동구 밖에서 노름판에서 모내기 새참 끝 보리밭에서

푸른 하늘에 보리 이삭이 점점이 박힐 때까지

각혈 같은 춤을 추는 여자

궁둥이에 흙을 털며 총총히 못줄을 잡으러 가는 여자

가을 들판에서 참새와 함께 마지막 벼 이삭을 거둘 줄 아는 여자

슬픔으로 꽃을 피울 줄 아는 여자

Bang An-Na

The Woman

Woman tasting like a broth of all the gossips boiled together overnight
Woman fermented like rice wine who wouldn't let go of a guy until dawn
Woman dancing like a shaman in front of all the people gathered including courtesans disguised as men for she failed to suppress special power inside
Woman dancing like a patient coughing up blood at the bar, at the outskirt
of the village, at the gambling house, at the barley field during the break
amid rice planting until barley ears are stuck in the blue sky
Woman who shakes the earth off the buttocks and works to plant rice
Woman who knows how to gather ears of rice at the field along with sparrows
Woman who knows how to bring forth flowers with sorrow

칼바람 부는 겨울 벌판에서도 사랑의 씨앗을 뿌릴 줄 아는 여자

봄 여름 가을 겨울 사계절 칭칭 동여매고

신내림 받는 여자, 그 여자

봄이 되면 열두 폭 치맛자락 흩날리며

들꽃 향기로 교향악을 연주할 줄 아는 여자

바람 같은 그 여자.

월간문학 소설 등단. 순수문학 시 등단. 신인문학상 수상. [블랭크][마지막 대화] 외

Woman who knows how to sow seeds of love even in the cold field of winter
Woman who wraps herself with cloth in all seasons
the same woman being possessed by a spirit
Woman who knows how to play symphonic music with the scent of grass flower
fluttering her skirt twelve-fold wide in the spring
The woman who is like the blowing wind

Made literary debut as a novelist through *Monthly Literature* and as a poet through winning the prize of new writer from Seonsoo Literature. Published books, *Blank, Last Dialogue*

백점숙

유빙

우리 사랑은
세월의 강 줄 타고
유빙 속에 박혀 오는데
어떻게 잊을까

소리쳐 부르면
한마디 말이 모자란 너
유빙에 얹어
있을 수 없는 미로
동행이 될까

건국대학교 정법대 정치외교학과 학사, 행정대학원 여성정책학과 석사, 미국 브리지포트 대학 교육학 박사 수료. 몬테소리학교 교사자격증. 2021년 한올문학으로 등단. 2023년 영랑문학상 해외작가 대상 수상. 현재 국제펜 이사, 순수문학 이사, 앵커리지 한인회 재정이사, 한국문인협회 회원.

Baik Jeum-Sook

Drift Ice

How can I forget
our love
stuck in drift ice
coming in time flowing like a river?

Calling you out loud
feeling short of a word to put
I wonder if you could be my companion
on drift ice broken apart and floating
in a unforgettable maze

Made literary debut through *Hanol Literature* in 2021. Northern Lights Preschool & Child Care, Creekwood Inn & RV Park, Alaska Korean News CEO. Member of The Korean Writers Association. Published poetry book *The Vacant Seat, Talks With Kids*, the collection of essays *My Fragmentary Thought* and a book in translation, *With A Stick in One Hand*, and more

백점숙

스퍼산 여신이여

스퍼산 여신이여
당신의 거친 숨결과
코비드(COVID-19) 후유증으로 아직도 움츠리고 있나이다

아름답고 평화롭게 잠자는 여인(Sleeping Lady)의
숨결 느끼며
꽃 망울 먹고 여름 꽃축제 준비하게 하시고
전쟁나간 낭군이 돌아올 때까지 만이라도
잠자는 여인이 평온을 찾게 해 주소서

알래스카를 품은 사랑의 연인이여
태양이 입 맞춘 푸른 바다를 보소서
당신의 거친 숨결 안에
세상 만물이 떨고 있나이다

Baik Jeum-Sook

Goddess of Mount Spurr

Goddess of Mount Spurr
We live still hunching our shoulders in fear
of your fiery breath and in the aftermath of COVID-19

Please feel the breath of beautiful Sleeping Lady in peaceful slumber
enjoy the flower buds growing for the summer festival
and keep Sleeping Lady resting in slumber
until her beloved comes back from battle

Goddess of Love embracing Alaska
Please take a look at the blue sea the sun kisses
and all the living things trembling in fear of your fiery breath

붉은 분노의 용암으로 산허리를 감싸고

하늘과 땅은 잿빛 연탄재로 숨통을 막았던

1953, 1992.

붉은 피 토해 당신의 분노 알게 하였으니

하늘, 인간, 자연의 삶이

공존해야 할 이유를 알고 있나이다

당신의 두 손 위에 나의 두 손 모아 자비를 노래하오니

고향 찾아 힘차게 물질하여 오고 있는

세먼 맞이하게 하여 주소서

당신의 너그럽고 아름다운 사랑을

영원히 우리 가슴에 품을 수 있도록 스퍼산 여신이여.

You have made your mighty warning twice in 1953 and 1992
with molten lava erupting from the volcano
flowing down the mountain slops,
toxic gasses covering the sky and the earth to choke us to death
and we have learned a lesson from the rage you revealed:
human beings, the sky and nature should coexist in harmony

Putting my hands on yours, asking for you grace,
I pray for the time that I could see salmons swim vigorously
against the current to come back to their home rivers

Goddess of Mount Spurr, please let us embrace your generous love
with our arms and keep it in our heart forever

서상문

사랑의 의미

당신 안에 한 송이 꽃으로 필 수만 있다면
나는 지상에서 가장 뜨거운 노래를 남기리라
함께 바라보는 푸른 하늘을
호수의 윤슬처럼 반짝 반짝
서로가 빛나는 환희로 채우리라

그대 뜨락에 새들의 평화가 내리고
님의 품속이라면
어느 날 서리 맞은 꽃잎처럼 내 젊음이 시든다 해도
나의 삶은 결코 헛되지 않으리
남은 생은 어제 같은 추억만으로도 살 수 있으리.

Suh Sang-Mun

The meaning of love

If I could bloom in you as a single flower
I would leave the hottest song on earth.

I would fill the blue sky we look at together
With the joy of shining each other like the sparkle of a lake.

If the peace of birds descends on your garden, and I am in your arms,
One day, even if my youth withers like a flower petal hit by frost,
My life will never be in vain
I could live the rest of my life with only nostalgic memories like yesterday.

President of the Korea Military Critics Association, Ph.D

서상문

사랑의 불꽃

그대가 나를 그대 곁에 잠시 머물다 갈 나그네라 여길지라도,
그대가 나를 한 순간 반짝이다 사라질 사랑의 신기루라 여길지라도,
어느 날 그대의 낡은 앨범 속의 빛 바랜 사진으로 사라질지라도,
그대의 기억속 망각의 저편으로 한 때의 님으로 묻혀 버릴지라도,
정말 내가 그대의 속절없는 웃음으로 사라질지라도
어찌 할 수 없는 일이 되겠지요
고통을 안고 내디딘 사랑의 발걸음이라면
어차피 모든 고통은 내게 있으니까요
하지만 내가 사랑을 위한 사랑을 마다하지 않는 한
그대는 내 가슴 속에 영원히 꺼지지 않는 불꽃으로 타오를 겁니다.

Suh Sang-Mun

Flame of Love

Even if you think of me as a traveler who will stay by your side for a while,
Even if you think of me as a mirage of love that will sparkle for a moment and then disappear,
Even if one day I disappear into a faded photo in your old album,
Even if I am buried in your memory as a former lover on the other side of oblivion,
Even if I disappear into your helpless laughter,
Even if I really disappear into your helpless laughter,
It's something I can't do anything about.
If it is a step of love that carries pain,
After all, all the pain is mine.
But as long as I don't give up love for love's sake,
You will burn in my heart as an undying flame that will never go out.

소명환

노모님과 함께

십일월 늦가을에 할미꽃 피어났네

저승에 계실 분을 꿈 속에서 만났는가

한번 지면 못 보실 꽃 시들까 두려우니

바람아 불지마라 시간도 멎어다오

월포 푸른 물결 아는 듯 잠잠하고

동해바다 수평선에 아침 해 찬란하네.

월간순수문학 등단. 고려대학교 대학원 졸업(농학박사). 부천대학교 식품영양학과 교수 정년퇴임. 한국식품영양학회 제16대 회장 역임. 한국식품영양학회 학술상 수상. 필동인회 회원. 한국문인협회 시분과 회원. 발효연구소 미림원 연구소장(현재).

So Myung-Hwan

With My Old Mother

In November, I saw a pasque flower happen to bloom in late autumn
Feeling odd as if I met a dead person again in my dream
I wished the wind to stop blowing and the time to stop running
being afraid of the flower getting withered if it once fell down
With blue waves at Wolpo Port staying calm as if they knew my mind
the morning sun was glowing bright on the horizon of the East Sea

---

Made literary debut through *Seonsoo Literature*. Ph.D. in agricultural science. Currently, director of Fermentation Research Center, Mirimwon. Former professor at Bucheon Univ. The 16th president of Korea Food and Nutrition Society. Received Korea Food and Nutrition Academy Award. Member of The Korean Writers Association & Member of coterie Phil.

소명환

서천 동백숲

입술연지 붉게 찍고 나들이 나온 겨울아씨
두툼한 초록 외투 윤기가 반들반들
동지섣달 찬바람에 누구를 기다리나
동박새 보고파서 겨울에야 오신 건가

하얀 테 안경 쓰고 폼 잡는 동박새
나비처럼 나폴 나폴 숨바꼭질하는 건가
서천 바다 칼바람이 동백정을 흔들어도
굳게 뻗은 가지 팔로 서로 품는 동백숲.

So Myung-Hwan

Camellia Forest at Seocheon

Winter ladies come out in thick green glossy coat
wearing red lipstick to the petals,
I wonder who they are waiting for in the cold wind
or if they come in the winter for they miss white-eyes

White-eyes wearing the rim of eye glasses show off their figure
lightly flying like butterflies playing hide-and-seek
In the frosty wind of the sea at Seocheon shaking a lonely pavilion
camellias hold themselves tight with strong branches making a forest

소융일

엄마의 강

하이얀 모시 적삼같이
미소 진
엄마 얼굴

깊은 주름에
잠긴 사연
강물처럼 흐르고

메아리진
그리움이
마음에 사무친다

어디선가
들리는 듯
엄마 목소리
가만히 눈을 감고 귀 기울인다

충남 논산 출신. 월간 순수문학 등단. 필동인 회원. (사) 한국문인협회 회원. 월간 순수문학 이사

So Yung-Il

Mother's River

Mother's face
with a gentle smile
like white ramie fabric

The traces of her life stories
inscribed in the deep wrinkles
are left flowing like river water

Longing for her
being echoed so much deep
in the heart

To the voice of my mother
coming from somewhere
I strain my ears
listening attentively with my eyes closed

Made literary debut through *Seonsoo Literature*. Member of The Korean Writers Association. Board member of Seonsoo Literature. Member of coterie Phil

소융일

낮에 나온 반달

한 점 구름 없는 쪽빛 창공
맑고 높은 가을 하늘
낮달이 혼자 서성거린다
지그시 한 눈 감고 누굴 기다리나

간밤에 홀로 두고 온 연인
차마 발길 돌릴 수 없어
오던 길 되돌아보다
길을 잃어 망부석이 되었나

별빛 쏟아지는 캠프파이어
활활 타는 장작불에
솜사탕 녹인 사랑
어쩌다 혼자되어 하염없이 서서

눈을 감아도 감아도 떠오르는
목화솜 같은
너의 눈빛 스며든 가슴 안고
오늘도 낮달 되어 너를 기다린다

So Yung-Il

Half Moon in the Daytime

With no cloud in the open air
somewhere in clear and high sky of the autumn
appears the moon in the daytime hovering alone
waiting for someone with the eyes closed

For a lover left alone last night
you couldn't have turned around
but lost your way and became a stone statue
while just looking back at your lover

In the starlight pouring down
your love so sweet like cotton candy melt away
in the burning firewood around a campfire;
you are left alone standing absentmindedly

With my eyes closed
but still having lingering feelings
of your eyes like fluffy cotton held in my heart
I become the hovering half moon waiting for you

손준식

삼월 거리에 나서면

만물 약동하는 소리
파도 치듯 밀려오면
내 마음 어찌할 바 모른다
삼월 거리에 나서면

메타세콰이어 나뭇가지
새순 맞을 채비하느라
단정히 이발도 했다

목련 꽃망울 위로
사알짝 아기 참새
입 맞춤 하는 한나절

사랑 움트는 소리
연두 나래 펴고
가슴 속 파고든다

―――――
서울문학 등단. 영랑문학상 우수상 수상. 시집 : 『어느 민들레의 삶』, 『나뭇잎 편지』

Son Jun-Shik

Coming out to the Streets of March

At the sounds of everything throbbing with life
coming in like rolling waves
I don't know what to do with my mind
standing on the streets of March

The branches of metasequoia trees
busy preparing for the buds growing
look tidy with all the hairy leaves trimmed

Baby birds kiss lightly
on the flowering buds of magnolias
during the daytime

The sounds of love burgeoning
with light green wings unfurled
make my heart flutter in joy

Made literary debut through *Seoul Literature*. Awarded Youngrang Literature Prize. Published poetry books *A Life of Dandelion*, *Letter of Tree Leaves*

손준식

황혼길에서

빛 바랜 황혼 길 들어서면
모두가 아름답게 보인다
야생화 이슬 머금은 모습에도
마음이 설레고
흘러가는 구름을 보아도
애틋한 정이 느껴진다

이 모두가 아쉬운 나의 생이기에

하늘 위 날아가는 철새 무리들
바라보는 눈가에
이슬 맺힌다
저 철새는 돌아가서 오는 길을 알건만
인생은 돌아오는 길 모르기에

Son Jun-Shik

On the Road in Twilight

Once you step into the twilight of life
everything looks beautiful
At the sight of dewdrops on wild flowers
your heart flutters in joy
Upon seeing the clouds floating idly
you feel your heart getting warm inside

Everything I see is a part of my life

Watching a flock of migrating birds
flying in the sky
I feel dewdrops in my eyes
for I don't know how to fly back home in life
unlike the migrating birds that know the way back home

송낙현

섬

바다 품에 안겨
날마다
자장가 들으니

나도
가끔은
섬이고 싶다

대구광역시 군위 출생. 『예술세계』〈시〉로 등단. 시집 『안개 속에 떠오르는 해』
(2023) 외 2권. 제28회 순수문학상 대상(2020) 외 다수 수상

Song Nak-Hyun

An Island

An island embraced in the ocean
Everyday
Listening to lullabies

Likewise
Sometimes
I wants to be the island

Made literary debut through *Art World*. Awarded The 28th Seonsoo Literature Prize and many more. Published poetry book *The Sun Rising in the Fog* (2023) and more

송낙현

어느 날 문득 깨닫다

겨울과 봄 사이

함께 살아온 많은 지인들이
마치 늦여름 매미가 뚝뚝 땅에
떨어지듯이 그렇게 떠나가는걸
애도하면서

'올림픽 경기에서의 마라톤은
일등이 최고이지만, 인생 마라톤에서는
꼴찌가 최고라는 것을'

어느 날 문득 깨닫다

Song Nak-Hyun

One Thing I Realized All of a Sudden

Between winter and spring

I have been offering my condolences
to many acquaintances I have known for long
who drop dead helplessly as if they were cicadas
falling down one by one in late summer

'In the Olympic marathon
winning the gold medal is the best
but the best in a marathon of life is to finish last'

That's one thing I realized all of a sudden one day

오정선

시를 읽는 소녀

무엇인가를 갈망하며 머리 숙여 다소곳이 시 구절에 푹 빠져
음미하는 여유로움을 만끽한 소녀의 모습 좋을씨고

파아란 하늘을 올려다 보노라니
흰구름은 솜이불이 되어 포근히 덮어 준 것 같아라

먹구름을 요로 깔지 말라고
난간 기둥에 기대어 앉아 즐거이 시를 읽는 소녀의
포동포동한 낯에 기도 소리도 새록새록 묻어나네.

제주 서귀포시 출생. 제주와 인천에서 행정직 공무원 다년 봉직. 순수문학인회 이사. 영주문학회 부회장. 제주한국문인 부회장. 등단: 한국문인(시), 순수문학(수필)

Oh Jeong-Seon

A Girl Reading a Poem

A girl indulging in reading a poem with longing for something
always looks beautiful, getting herself relaxed

Looking up at the blue sky would make her wonder
if white clouds looking like cotton comforter could cover her cozily

Rejecting to use dark clouds as bedding, the girl with chubby cheeks sitting against the railing post enjoys reading poetry as if making a prayer with her voice fresh and pure

---

Made literary debut as a poet through Korean Writers & as an essayist through *Seonsoo Literature*. Vice-president of Jeju Korean Writers Association. Board member of Seonsoo Literature Association. Vice-president of Youngju Literature Association.

오정선

빈터

널브러진 빈터에 우거진 잡초는 베임을 당하여도 시간이
지나면 빗물을 마시고 쑥쑥 자라나 여전히 주인 행세를 하고

잡석(雜石)은 여기저기 산만하게 나뒹굴며 웃는 듯 하여라

저 빈터가 사유지가 아니라 공유지라야 마땅하고
옳은 것이라는 생각에 잠겨본다

저 빈터를 잘 일구어 상추씨, 시금치씨, 유채씨를
뿌리면 멀지 않아 싹을 틔우고

부지런한 손은 우리네의 식탁을 더욱 풍성하게 할진대
우리네가 품은 생각이 실현되게 경작하여 주소서

도심 속의 금싸라기 같은 저 빈터는 오늘도 나를 쳐다보며 말
을 거는 것처럼 반가워하니 마음도 흥겹도다.

Oh Jeong-Seon

A Vacant Lot

Weeds cut short in a vacant lot grow back thriving in rain after a while and become predominant

Rubble stones are scattered around disorderly, looking as if laughing at me

It occurs to my mind that the vacant lot should be public property, not private

Sowing the seeds for lettuce, spinach, canola to sprout and grow in the lot

The vegetables would make a rich and plentiful dinner in good hands,
so I wish and I hope to see the wish becomes reality

I feel good today for the vacant lot left yet in the downtown seems to be delighted to see me and tries to talk to me.

오종민

레테
- 망각의 강

잊고 싶지 않은 기억과
잊어서는 안 될 중요한 사실들은
돌아서면 잊혀지곤 하는데

그때 우리 그렇게 헤어지고 난 후
몸부림을 쳐 보아도 잊을 길 없어
끝없이 방황하는 발걸음 멈추지 못하고

그 강을 건너면 모든 것이 잊혀진다기에
그곳으로 가는 길을 물으니
죽음의 강 간너편에 있단다

그것이 사랑이었을까
그렇다면 우리의 사랑은
죽어서야 완성되는 비극이었던 것일까.

*레테(Lethe): 그리스 신화에 나오는 망각의 강.

한국문인협회, 한국현대시인협회, 국제계관시인연합한국본부, 국제PEN한국본부, 필동인, 문예춘추 회원. 영랑문학상 수상. 고려대학교 영어영문학과 졸업. ㈜선경(現SK) 과장. ㈜갑을 부장, 충남방적㈜ 베트남 호찌민 영업소장 역임, 시집:「노을」

Oh Jong-Min

Lethe
- The river of oblivion

Memories wanted not to be forgotten and
Important things that shouldn't be forgotten
Are often forgotten when I turn around,
But after we broke up like that,
There's no way to forget no matter how hard I struggle.
So I can't stop my wandering steps.

They say, everything will be forgotten after crossing the river;
So I asked for the direction, and
They said it's on the other side of the river of death.

Was that a love?
If so, was our love a tragedy
That could only be completed after death?

오종민

추억 · 2

바위라도 뚫을 것 같던 젊은 날의 혈기
죽음과도 바꿀 것 같던 무모한 사랑

그 모든 것들이 떠나가 버린 뒤
이제 남겨진 것이라곤
잊으려 할수록 되살아나는 지난 추억뿐

오는 길에 흩뿌려진 아련한 추억들은
어느새 바람처럼 바짝 뒤쫓아와
휑한 가슴속을 훑어 지나간 뒤
다시 서글픈 그리움으로 다가와

날이 갈수록 화려한 빛을 잃어 가지만
오히려 윤곽이 또렷해지는
흑백사진으로 되살아나는 듯.

Oh Jong-Min

Memories · 2

Youthful vigor that seemed to pierce even a rock.
A reckless love that'd be exchanged for death.

The only thing left is the memories after everything's gone,
Which comes back to life the more I try to forget.

The faint memories scattered behind
Suddenly follows me like wind before I know it,
Sweep through my empty heart and comes again as a sad longing.

They are gradually losing their former charm, but
It seems that they revive as black-and-white photos,
Making the outline clearer.

오현정

오늘

지금이 가장 좋은 때

첫 해산 후 숲길 걷는
지금이 가장 좋은 때

이제까지의 부끄러움 다 가려주는
활엽수가 친구하자는
지금이 가장 좋은 때

오후의 햇살이 남은 꿈을 찾아드는
지금이 가장 좋은 때

나는 어리석었지만 지혜를 찾아다닌 詩人

지금 이 순간이 고통의 詩를 빚는 행복한 시간

먼 길 돌아 다시 출발점에 서있는
지금 여기 그대 함께라면

오늘이 내 가장 좋은 때

Oh Hyun-Jung

Today

This is the best time

Walking along the woods after one's first childbirth
This is the best time

Shadowing all the shame thus far
Broad-leaved trees wanting to be my friend
This is the best time

Afternoon sunshine flying to the rest of my dream
This is the best time

I am a fool poet, but seeking wisdom

This right moment a happy time creating a poem of pain

Now standing back at the starting point after a long way
With you this right moment

Today is the best time of my life

오현정

반구정伴鷗亭

사목리로 돌아와 갈매기와 화답하던
햇살 좋은 날이면 강변 솔밭 언덕 위로 굽이치는
임진강 푸른 물결에 송악산 바람을 맞이하던

청정문淸政門 들어서는 숭모의 발길에
황희님 혼결 불러주는 단아한 단청
의연한 정자亭子 너머

멀리 있는 한 핏줄도
청백리淸白吏, 읊는 시구詩句에
그리운 사람 찾아
눈썹 하얗게 달려오는 그 곳

경북 포항 출생. 숙명여대 불문과 졸업. 1978년, 1989년 『현대문학』 2회 추천완료로 등단. 시집 『지금이 가장 좋은 때』 『몽상가의 턱』 『라데츠키의 팔짱을 끼고』 『광교산 소나무』 『고구려 남자』 『봄온다』 『에스더 편지』 『물이 되어, 불이 되어』 『마음의 茶 한 잔 · 기타 詩』 『보이지 않는 것들을 위하여』 『리나, 고마워』 등. 한국문협 작가상, PEN문학상, 영랑문학상, 애지문학상, 숙명문학상, 김기림문학상대상 등을 수상. 역임: 한국비평가협회 부회장, 한국여성문학인회 부이사장, 한국문인협회 이사, 한국시인협회 이사. 현재: 국제PEN한국본부 자문위원, 숙명여대 문인회 회장.

Oh Hyun-Jung

The Resting Place of a Gull

A resting place where seagulls respond in singing
A breeze winds its way through a pine forest
The wind blowing from Songak Mountain turns a bend
On a river of Imjin on a bright day

On the step of admirer entering the resting place
Various colors on a clean door invoke the soul of Whang-hee

The spirits a long way off
Comes here out of love for the verse read by
A government official
It is the place one burns with passion

Pohang-si, Gyengsangbuk-do, Korea Graduate from French Language and Literature of Sookmyung Women's University. In 1978, 1989, debut on 「Hyundae Munhak」 through the completion of two recommendations . Poetry 「Now is the best time」 「The Dream of Dreamer」 「With Radetzky's cheeks on」 「Gwanggyo-san pine tree」 「The man of goguryeo」 「Spring comes」 「Be water, Be fire」 「Letters of esther」 「In the heart of a cup of tea and others」 「For things that don't see」 「Rina, thank you」 etc. International P.E.N. Literary Award Yeong-rang Literary Award, Ae-ji Literary Award, Kim G-rim Literary Sookmyung university Literay Award, etc. Former vice-president of Korea Criticism Association, President of Korea Women Writers Association, Director of The Korean Writer's Association, Former Director of The Korea Poets Association, Advisory Committee member Director of International P.E.N. Korea Center, Director in Korean Women Writer's Association, President of Sookmyung Women's University Writer's Alumni Association.

유장희

격랑(激浪)

세상이 격랑이라면
내 몸은 가냘픈
한 쪽의 나뭇잎
물결이 아무리 거세도
나는 뒤집힐 일 없네

세상이 격랑이라면
내 영혼은 소리 없는
한 결의 바람
물결이 아무리 높아도
나는 떨어질 일 없네

세상이 격랑이라면
내 삶은 나긋한
한 줄기 물 풀
물결이 아무리 빨라도
나는 휩쓸릴 일 없네

Yoo Jang-Hee

Heavy Seas

The world is called heavy seas
Then my body is a little leaf
Though the wave is rampant
My body will stay as is

The world is called heavy seas
Then my soul is a little breeze
with no noise
No matter how high it is
My body will stay as is

The world is called heavy seas
Then my life is a soft sea weed
No matter how fast the wave is
My body will stay where it was

세상이 격랑이라도
내 바램은 별것이 아니네
그냥 모두가 부르는
흔한 노래라네

파도를 넘어
조용한 초원을 찾아
영원히 쉴곳에
안착하는 것이라네

순수문학 등단, 필동인회 회원, 한국문인협회 회원, KIEP 원장, 이화여대 부총장, 국민경제 자문회의 부의장, POSCO 이사회 의장, 동반성장 위원장, 국제로타리 3650 총재, (현)국가원로회의 공동의장, (현)매일경제 고문, (현) 대한민국학술원 회원

The world is called heavy seas
Then my hope is only a whistle
Like a quite sonata
that people love to sing

Over the big wave
Looking for a soft meadow
My soul will stop the journey
Resting in peace of eternity

유장희

시인되기

경제학은 시인의 몫이다
인간은 물질로만으로
행복하지 못한다
아리스토텔레스가 말한대로
인간은 사회적 동물이라
혼자는 살 수 없다

가족이 있고 친구가 있고 이웃이 있다
가족과 친구와 이웃이 불행하면
나만의 행복이 의미가 없다
내 주변이 행복해야
나도 행복하다

시인은 예술가다
주변의 일들을 소상히 살피면서
예쁘고 아름답고 신선하고 감동적인
느낌을 채취하여
글로 그림을 그린다
영감(靈感)이 문화(文化)로 전달된다

Yoo Jang-Hee

Becoming a Poet

Economics is the poet's share.
Only through materials
humans can't be fulfilled.
As Aristotle stated,
humans are social beings
who can't live alone.

Family, friends, and neighbors live together.
If my family, friends and neighbors are unhappy,
my happiness is meaningless.
When they are happy,
I become happy.

Poet is an artist.
Noticing things around you with keen eyes,
digesting the beautiful, fresh
and touching feelings,
compose a picture by letters.
Inspiration is transformed into culture.

경제학의 목표가 행복이라면
영감의 문화로 이웃을 감동시키면
나를 넘어 주변을 아름답게 채색하면
그는 바로 시인이다

냉철한 머리와 뜨거운 가슴
알프레드 마샬이 백번 옳다
경제학자들이여
먼저 시인이 되라

If the objective of economics is happiness,
inspirational culture touches neighbors and
beautifully paints vicinity beyond your surroundings,
that is the poet.

"Cool-heads but warm hearts,"
Alfred Marshall is absolutely right.
Dear economists,
foremost, be a poet.

혜림 윤수자

봄날의 편지

남촌에서 날아오는 바람
나지막하게 깔리니 봄길이 된다

봄볕 한자락은 풀잎에 깔고
이슬비로 흙먼지 털어내니

노랑 꽃잎 애기씨들
연못가에 앉아 노니네

수중거울 들여다 보며
옷 매무새 가다듬고

바람결에 님 부르는 손짓으로
배시시 웃는데

휘리릭 지나가는 그림자에
님인가 돌아보니

하얀 나비 나풀거리며 지나가네

월간 순수문학 시 등단. 순수문학인협회 회원. 글벗문학회원. 일본 동경 서도예술학회 초대그룹전시회. 한국 국제살롱전 초대작가.

Yoon Sou-Ja(Hyerim)

A Letter of the Spring

The wind blows from the south
laying itself down paving the road of spring

Putting a streak of sunlight on a grass leaf
wiping off clay dusts with the drizzling rain

For fair maidens with yellow petals unfurled
sitting by the pond to enjoy the spring

Looking into the mirror of the pond
the maidens adjust their dress

Calling for lover in the breeze
they make bashful smiles with soft gestures

At a shadow going past so fast
the maidens turn around expecting to see their lover

But there is only a butterfly passing by, fluttering in the air

---

Made literary debut through *Seonsoo Literature*. Member of Seonsoo Literature Association & Writing Friends Literature Association. Quest writer of Korea for International Salon Exhibition. Participated in Group Exhibition Invited by Calligraphy art Society in Tokyo, Japan.

혜림 윤수자

모시 이불

노화 되지 않는
익어가는 사랑으로

물 처럼 움직이며
썩지 않는 사랑으로

밀물처럼 소리 없이
스며든다면

함께 바라보는 곳으로
손잡고 걸어 가리

쉽게 끓어오르지 않는
쉽게 식지 않는 그런 사랑

파아란 바람 타고
날아든다면

밤바람 속 별을 헤며
같은 곳 바라보는 님에게

풀먹인 모시 이불
덮어 드리리

Yoon Sou-Ja(Hyerim)

Ramie Blanket

With love getting matured
not aging

With love flowing like water
not being rotten

Towards the same direction we look together
I will walk holding your hands

Love neither boiling easily
nor cooling down so soon

If that kind of love comes to me
in the blue wind

Over that lover counting the number of the stars
while looking towards the same direction at night

I will place a ramie blanket
starched clean and straight

仁步 윤주홍

가을 無題(무제)

보라매 숲길 따라
바람이 걸어간다

뒤따라 가을 혼자
낙엽을 밟는 소리

寂寂(적적)히
쌓인 깊이에
흐르는 세월 소리

의학박사. 고려대 의대 졸업. 한국문인협회, 국제PEN한국본부 회원. 순수문학인협회 이사. 제14회 영랑문학상 대상 수상.

Yoon Ju-Hong

Autumn Untitled

Along the trail of Boramae forest
the wind blows as if strolling

The crunching sounds
autumn makes as if stepping on dry leaves

Being accumulated in quiet loneliness
the sounds of time flow
at the bottom of the autumn

M.D. Ph.D. in medicine from Korea Medical School. Member of The Korean writers Association. board member of Seonsoo Literature Association. Awarded The 14th Youngrang Literature Prize.

仁步 윤주홍

진달래

그리움 맺힌 사연 그리도 주체 못해
목놓아 울다울다 선혈(鮮血)로 물들이고
그 응혈(凝血)
꽃으로 폈나
정인의 치마 폭에

Yoon Ju-Hong

Azaleas

With the stories of longing suppressible no more
Crying their eyes out suffering in pains
Azaleas spit up blood clots
Turning into the flowers blooming
On the wide long skirt of their lover

윤호용

다섯 손가락

엄지 손가락은 문서이다
도장을 대신하여
엄지 인장을 찍고
엄지척하면 끝이다

손바닥은 종이이다
검지 손가락이 펜이 되어
손바닥에 싸인을 하면
둘 만의 약속이 된다

중지 손가락은 교만이다
가장 길다고 자랑하여
펼쳤다하면 욕이 되어
봉변을 당한다

약지 손가락은 영원이다
변치 않는 금빛 링을
약지 손가락에 끼우면
영원한 하나가 된다

Yun Ho-Yong

Five Fingers

The thumb can be used to verify documents
Instead of using an official stamp
press the thumb applied with ink
to authenticate the document

The palm can be used like a paper
Use the index finger like a pen
to sign on the palm
making a promise between two persons

The middle finger can signify arrogance
As the longest among the fingers
it's often used to express anger or disgust to someone
Don't use it unless you want to invite trouble

The ring finger always signifies endless commitment
If two lovers share a pair golden rings
on the ring finger
it means that the two lovers are meant to be together
forever

손가락은 약속이다
새끼 손가락을 마주 걸고
변치말자 다짐하는 약속이다

월간 순수문학 등단. 알래스카 은혜와 평강 순복음교회 담임목사. 알래스카 교회 연합회 회장. 저서 '알래스카에서 하나님 나라를 꿈꾸다'

The little finger or so-called pinky symbolizes a promise
People make a pinky swear
when they promise to do something no matter what

Made literary debut through *Seonsoo Literature*. Pastor in charge of Grace and Peace Full Gospel Church oin Alaska. President of Church United Association in Alaska. Published *Dream of a Country of God in Alaska*

윤호용

서커스(Circus) 인생

옛날 알던 서커스가 아니다
많은 동물들이 등장하던
그 때가 좋았고
그 곳에 부모의 추억이 있다

많은 동물이 나와야 기분이 좋고
땡그랑, 짤랑 소리와 조명에
주위 사람들의 시선이 향한다

요란한 듯 고요하고, 분주한 듯 질서 있고
발걸음을 재촉하는 화려한 불빛은
의심의 눈초리가 가시지 않는다

긴장된 마음으로 줄을 당기며
열정을 다하는 서커스 인생들의 삶이
감추인 내 삶의 끼를 읽힌다

Yun Ho-Yong

Life is a Circus

It is not the circus I used to know
I liked the one I remember
having many animals on the show
for it makes me recall the time with my parents

With many animals performing various tricks
the audience could have enjoyed the noisy show
with all the attentions focused under the stage lighting

Clamorous yet silent, disorganized yet orderly shows
were performed under the flamboyant lighting
making the audience excited and suspicious of the tricks they saw

Watching the acrobats doing their best with passion
pulling a rope with the mind strained
I thought I had the same kind of talent hidden inside me

올 때는 미소와 설렘 가득한 구경꾼 인생들이
갈 때는 피곤과 아쉬운 미련만 가득한 채 막을 내린다

고가 마비된 인생들이 돌고 돌아
서로를 울리고 웃기는 서커스 광대 인생이 되고
그 때가 좋았던 서커스 인생이 내가 된다

The audience coming in smile and with fluttering heart left the circus with lingering emotions after the curtain falls

Our lives going round and round become the life of clowns
who sometimes make us cry or make fun of us;
I know the life I enjoyed at the circus has become a part of me

이금희

편지

일등항해사로
처음 원양어선을 타고
요코하마항을 떠나면서
배 위에서 쓴
너의 편지를 받았다

아득한 그 바다 위에서
별이 내리던 그 밤에
너의 꿈을 그리며

가장 가까이 생각나는
한 사람에게
편지를 쓴다고 했다

그 편지는
푸른 바다위를 날아
육지에 닿아
소녀의 작은 손에
전해졌다

Lee Keum-Hee

A Letter

When you first boarded the deep-sea fishing vessel
As a chief mate
And departed from Yokohama Port,
You wrote a letter on the ship
And I received it.

On that vast ocean,
On the night that stars rained down,
Dreaming of your dream

You said
You were writing a letter to the one
Who felt closest to your heart

The letter
Flew across the blue sea,
Reached the land
And was delivered
To the little girl's hands.

바다 위에서 보낸
그 편지에는
"YOKOHAMA"라는 항구이름 외에
발신인 주소가 없었다

그 편지에 대한 답장은
끝내 전달할 수 없었지

경주 출생. 서강대 경영대학원 졸업 (경영학석사). 프랑스 원자력회사 FRAMEX 근무. 한전 원자력 프로젝트 통번역 참여. 한국고속철도건설 프로젝트 통번역 참여. KDNUAE프로젝트 통번역 참여. 2014인천아시안게임 통역지원 . 2020〈서울문학〉 외국어문학 번역시인 등단. 2024〈순수문학〉 시인 등단

The letter you sent from the sea
Bore only the port name
"YOKOHAMA"
Without a sender's address

The reply to that letter
Could never be delivered.

Born in Gyeongju. Graduated from Kyeongbuk National University (Major: French Language & Literature, Minor: English Language & Literature). Graduated from Sogang University Business School(MBA). worked for French Nuclear Power Company, FRAME X. Participated in translation for Korea High-Speed Rail Construction Project, KEPCO Nuclear Power Project, KDNUAE Project, Participated in 2014 Incheon Asian Games as interpreter. Debut as a translator poet of foreign literature in Seoul Literature Magazine. Debut as a poet in Soonsoo Literature Magazine

이금희

고별전

내가 살고 있는 일산 신도시
한 대형 쇼핑몰이 문을 닫았다

개점 29주년이 되는 올해,
폐업 한 달을 앞두고
고별전을 한다고
문자를 보내왔다

나는 이곳에 10년 넘게 살고 있고
전철역에서 가까워
자주 이용하던 곳이라
아쉬움이 컸다

행사 기간 동안 두어 번 들러
몇 가지 필요한 물건을 샀다

그리고 마지막날,
나는 그곳을 다시 찾았다
사람들이 여전히 붐비고
비워지는 매장마다 아쉬운 듯
물건을 고르고 있었다

Lee Keum-Hee

Farewell Event

One large shopping mall in Ilsan
Where I've been living, was closed.

This year marks the 29th anniversary of its opening.
A month before the closure,
It sent a text saying
That it was having a farewell event.

I've been living here over 10 years
As it was close to the subway station,
I used it often
So I was very disappointed.

I stopped by a couple of times during the event
To buy a few necessary items

And on the last day,
I went there again
People were still busy
And picked out items
As if they felt sorry for each empty store

각 층마다 빼곡하게 물건들로
가득 찼던 매장들은
빈 매대만 덩그러니 남기고
이별의 순간을 맞이하고 있었다

이곳에서 영화도 보고
계절마다 옷도 사고
기념일에는 선물도 사고
맛있는 음식으로 외식도 했던
나의 추억도 조용히 닫혀 갔다

오랜 시간 함께했던
G백화점을 나오면서
아쉬움과 애잔함, 왠지 모를 슬픔이
밀려와 한번 더 뒤돌아보았다

어둠 속에 말없이 서 있는
이 커다란 덩치의 건물도 그곳을 다녀간
수많은 사람들의
웃음과 즐거움과 추억을 기억할까?

The stores, which were packed with goods
On each floor,
Were facing a moment of farewell,
Leaving only empty shelves.

My memories of watching movies here,
Buying seasonal clothes,
Buying gifts on anniversaries,
Eating out with delicious food,
Have been quietly closing.

As I walked out of the G department store
Where I had been for so long,
I felt regret, sadness and an unknown sorrow,
And looked back once more.

Does this huge building
Standing silently in the darkness
Remember the laughter, joy and memories
Of the countless people who have been there?

이행자

썩고지고 죽고지고

옥합을 깨뜨린 마리아처럼
나의 긴 머리 풀어
당신의 발을 씻는
꿈을 꾸지만

가련한 나의 신부야

손 내미신 당신은
영원한 나의 친구

썩기 위해 죽었더니
성령 충만 은사의 옷을 입혀
통곡하며 춤을 추네

이 썩을 것이
썩지 아니함을 입다니
왠일인가요

1994년 문예한국으로 등단. 한국문인협회 이사. 영순회 이사

Lee Haeng-Ja

Turning to Dust Again In the Holy Spirit

As Maria did when she broke an alabaster jar
to wash Jesus's feet with the oil
I dream about offering myself to wash your feet
with my long hair

My poor bride, you called me

With your hands reaching out to me
you became my friend forever

Embracing the death to turn to dust again
makes me blessed in spiritual words
crying for the Grace, dancing in the Holy Spirit

Wondering about His Will
for me being blessed
of eternal life

이행자

현충일 동작동에서

그때 그렇게
두고 간 정열이
빨간 장미로 머무는 아침

십오 년을 흐르는
노모의 눈물은
누이의 흰 블라우스를 적신다

작은 비석은
거대한 사열대를 이루는데
그때
그 전쟁의 포성이
메아리 되는 곳

고엽을 앓는 전우가
다리를 절며
오천여 비석의
고랑을 헤매고 있다

Lee Haeng-Ja

At the National Cemetery on a Memorial Day

The compassion
having been left behind in the past day
is now turned into a red rose of the morning

The tears of an old mother
who has been crying for fifteen years since her son left
made wet the white blouse of the dead soldier's sister

Small granite headstones in the cemetery
are placed in the rows, appearing uniform
like soldiers are lined up for a parade
where we can still hear the roaring sounds
of the guns and cannons fired at a war

Where survived veterans
suffering the effects of exposure to defoliants
are limping around, wandering among the headstones
of his fellow soldiers died in a battle

小花 이현채

진달래 피었구나

두견의
넋이 담긴
진달래 연분홍 꽃
이른 봄
서둘러서
봄 맞이 꽃 피우니
번지는
꽃 웃음 물결
동산 가득 번져야
소화의
순정 심어
가꿔온 꿈의 동산
올해도
어김 없이
움트고 꽃피우니
들새들
제 둥지인 듯
잠시 들려 휴식을

Lee Hyun-Chae

Azaleas Blooming

Azaleas
containing the soul
of the cuckoo in sorrow
hasten to bring forth
the flowers
blooming in early spring
spreading floral smiles
rolling like waves
all over the hill
presenting a spring scenery
of the hill cultivated
with pure love of mine
This year, too, without fail,
azalea flowers
sprout and bloom
where wild birds
take a rest
feeling home in the nests

小花 이현채

진통

봄꽃들
제 시간 맞춰
예쁜 꽃 피우기 위해

긴 겨울 잠에서 깨어나
새 생명 출산 무언의 진통은

아무리
모진 혹한 막으려 해도 어림도 없지

사랑 또한 봄꽃처럼
아름다울거야

대구 출생. 월간 순수문학 등단. 호산대 졸. 호산대학 동문회장 역임. 담수회 여성회원.

Lee Hyun-Chae

Labor Pains

Spring flowers
try to bloom
on time

Awakening from a long winter sleep
quietly risking labor pains for a new life

In spite of bitter coldness
nothing can stop their burgeoning

Love also would be like spring flowers
manifesting such a beauty

Made literary debut through *Seonsoo Literature*. Graduated Hosan Univ. Former president of Hosan Univ. Alumni. Member of Damsoo Society.

임병숙(임이랑)

멋진 노년의 미소

세월을 품고
웃음 띤 얼굴로
노을 앞에 모였네

은발 휘날리며
옛 추억 서린
소년 소녀들 모여
사진 한 장 찍고

품격을 거울로
도도하게
주름진 얼굴을 다듬네

"하나도 안 변했네"
거짓말도 반가운
맑은 하늘 빛

1999년 월간 순수문학 등단. 한국문인협회, 국제PEN 회원. 한국여성문학인회 이사. 시집 '하얗게 하루가 열리는 소리' 외

Im Byung-Sook

Beautiful Smiles at Old Age

Embracing time in the arms
with faces smiling
we gathered before the sunset

With gray hair swaying in the wind
boys and girls of the past gathered
with the memories
to take a picture together

Posing in front of a mirror
with the wrinkled faces
polished in grace and elegance

"You haven't changed a bit," someone says,
and we are all pleased to hear even such a lie
in the sunlight so much clear and bright

Made literary debut through *Seonsoo Literature* in 1999. Member of The Korean Writers association & PEN International, Korea Center. Board member of Korea Women Writers Association. Published poetry book *The Sounds of a Day Opening in White*

임병숙(임이랑)

꽃처럼 나도

나쁜 말은 속으로 삭이고
조용히 기쁨을 흘리면 좋겠다

나도 향기를 품고
고운 자태면 좋겠다

넘어져 흉터 많아도
꽃을 닮아 예쁘면 좋겠다.

Im Byung-Sook

Me Being Like Flowers

Swallowing bad words
I'd like to give out joy in silence

Keeping the fragrance inside
I'd like to have the graceful figure

Even with many scars made by falling
I'd like to look pretty like flowers

정도병

굿샷

잔디 양탄자가 끝없이 펼쳐진
치앙마이 하이랜드 페어웨이

산으로 둘러친 초원 위에서
햇빛이 미끄러진다
풀 향기 바람에 실려와 코끝을 간질인다

긴 그리움이
홀마다 하얀 깃발이 되어 손을 흔들고 있다
호수 위 분수는 폭죽을 터트린다

그린 둘레에는 어김없는 모래 벙커들
드높은 담벼락을 탈출하는 기막힌 스킬
홀인 순간
부딪치는 다국적 손바닥들

Jung Do-Byung

Good Shot

The green fairway of Highland golf course in Chiang Mai
stretched out like endless carpet

On the green fields surrounded by the mountains
the sunlight came down slanting
with the scent of grasses in the wind tickling the nose

A white flag on a pole was stuck at the hole cup
wavering in the wind like our longing
while water jetted from the fountains in the lake

Playing out of the hazard area
with sand bunkers near the fairway
I felt thrilled when I made a hole-in-one
followed by enthusiastic congratulations from various
nationals

팔순맞이 가족 골프대회
치앙마이 하이랜드
2025년 1월 30일

아들이 만들어 준 총천연색 플래카드가
카메라 앞에서 춤을 춘다

함박웃음
파이팅!

월간 순수문학 등단. 한국문인협회, 필동인. 순수문학인협회 이사로 활동. 순수문학상 본상 수상. 시집 '내 안에 출렁이는 빛'

Family Golf Meeting for 80th Anniversary in Highland, Chiang Mai
Jan. 30, 2025

A colorful banner for family event prepared by my son
was in the wind wavering pleasantly

With big smiles
all of us had a jolly good time!

Made literary debut through *Seonsoo Literature*. Member of Korean Writers Association & Board member of Seonsoo Literature Association. Awarded Seonsoo Literature Prize. Published poetry book *Light Rolling inside Me*

정도병

물왕호

호수야
가슴 활짝 연
물왕호야

반짝이는 햇살 피어나고

산 그림자 드리운 수면
늘어진 실버들 사이로
물결 타는 청둥오리 가마우지

물왕호야
갈대숲 속삭이는 호수야
긴 의자에 걸터앉은 나는 가슴이 저려라

큰 호수 얼굴

눈 감으면 수면에 떠오는
어른거리는 보고픈 사람아
그리워라 혼자 그리워라

Jung Do-Byung

Mulwang Lake

A large area of water surrounded by land
With the chest open quite widely
Oh, Lake Mulwang

With the sunlight glittering in waves

On the surface with the floating shade of a mountain
Mallards and cormorants swim gently
Through willow branches hanging over the water

Oh, lake Mulwang
Watching reed forest whispering to you
I feel my heart ache, sitting astride on a bench

The face of a large lake

With my eyes closed
I still see the people I miss so much,
Glimmering on the surface of the lake

달밤 별밤에도
마음 맑은 사람아

헤매노라

찾아 헤매노라

At the moonlit night with the stars shining bright
I miss the person of clean mind

Wandering around

Wandering around and around to find the right one

정연수

강릉 커피

강릉, 그 이름을 입안에서 굴리다 보면
가릉가릉 솔잎을 흔드는 바람처럼

먼저 등을 보인 그대가 손을 내밀듯
비는 먼 곳에서부터 내린다

아무리 낡은 것이라도
그리움만큼 낡았으랴

살다 보면, 나만 흔들린 건 아닌 게다
명상을 깨고 나온 물방울들

파도 소리 내며 커피 끓는 주전자
그대를 한 잔 내리는 중이다.

문학박사, 「다층」 등단, 시집 「여기가 막장이다」, 「한국탄광시전집」, 산문집 「탄광촌 풍속 이야기」, 「노보리와 동발」, 「석탄산업유산 현황과 세계유산화 방안」, 「한국탄광사」, 「강원의 명소 재발견」 등, 24회 영랑문학상 평론 대상 수상.

Jeong Yeon-Soo

Gangneung Coffee

As I roll the name 'Gangneung' in my mouth,
Like the wind shaking pine needles,
the sound of 'ka-reung ka-reung' comes through.

Just as you turned your back and reached out,
The rain falls from a distant sky.

No matter how worn or old,
Can anything be as aged as longing itself?

As I live, I realize
I'm not the only one who shakes.
The droplets breaking the stillness of medi-tation,

Like the sound of waves, the kettle hums and boils.
I pour you a cup,
A taste of you, in this steaming brew.

정연수

정동진 일출

숲이 묵언 수행 들어가듯, 탄광이 문을 닫던 날
그날도 해는 떴다

채탄부 굴진부 선탄부 버력처럼 버려지고
기차의 슬픈 바퀴는 눈물을 굴렸다

연탄처럼 잘 구워진 해는 따뜻한데
화력 좋은 푸른 갱구는 입을 다물었다

모래시계가 해안선을 돌아 나오는 사이
배우를 닮은 관광객이 찾아온다

정동진이 탄광촌이었대
파도가 푸른 귀를 열어도 믿지 못하겠다고

캄캄한 막장도 순식간에 뚫어내던
광부가 살아서 더 아름다운 곳.

Jeong Yeon-Soo

Jeongdongjin Sunrise

The forest, entering silence like a monk in meditation,
The mine closes its doors that day too,

And still, the sun rises.
The coal fields, the drill teams,
Thrown away like an old relic,
While the sad wheels of the train roll on, shedding tears.

The sun, baked as warmly as briquettes,
But the strong blue mines' mouth stays sealed tight.

As the hourglass turns,
Tourists like actors arrive.

They say Jeongdongjin was once a mining town,
But even when the waves open their blue ears, they won't believe it.

The dark shaft that could be pierced in an instant,
A place made more beautiful by the miners who still live.

조대연

비워 내림

비워 내림을 알게 되었을 때
가장 아름다운 단풍빛으로 빛나고 있었어

고난의 세월에
푸르름도 있었고 성장도 있었지만
가장 진한 고움으로 무르익었을 때
이제 그 모두를 내려놓아야 해

훌훌 벗어 던지고
티끌 하나까지도 남음이 없을 때가
가장 자유로운 순간일 수가 있어

이젠 편안해져
시간까지도 날려 보내고
그 끝단에 이르러
그림자의 흔적도 지워 버려야지

Cho Dae-Yeun

Emptying Down

When I came to know the meaning of emptying down
I could see tinged maple leaves glowing most beautifully

In hard times
you can grow up flourishing in green
but sometimes you have to put everything down
when you get matured with splendid beauty

After taking off everything you wear
until the time you have nothing left
you can seize the moment you can be really free

Getting easy with everything around
even becoming free from the shackle of time
I will finally reach the end of nothing
erasing the trace of my own shadow

그렇게 내내 공(空) 속에서 머물다가
새순으로 다시 돌아오는 날
너의 모습 닮아서
영원의 빛으로 다시 태어날 거야.

I will stay in the void as long as it takes
until I can come back as a new sprout
having the look quite similar to you, then,
to be born again as the light lasting forever

조대연

불갑사 꽃무릇 길

불갑사 꽃무릇 길 걸어 봐요
달빛수상길 힘겹게 넘어와야만
그 꽃 수변에서 아름답게 반짝여 핌을 보지요

하지만 화려하고 아름다운
선운사 꽃도 질 때는
바람결 한점이면 쉬이 지고 말지요

꽃들은 그렇게 피고 지는데
당신을 잊고 산 날들이 무상하여서
빠르게 흘러간 지난 세월이
어느덧 꽃이 질 즈음이지요

Cho Dae-Yeun

The Path Full of Red Spider Lilies near Bulgapsa Temple

Take a walk along the path near Bulgapsa Temple
Once you cross over the moonlight deck with a little difficulty
you will see beautiful red spider lilies blooming by the reservoir

But beautiful and flamboyant flowers
blooming at Seonunsa Temple
fall so helplessly as well even in the gentle wind

While the flowers fall down and bloom again
I have lived in meaningless life, being unaware of you
Now, after the time fleeting so fast
I already see the seasonal close with the flowers about to fall

당신은 저 꽃으로
내 안에 피어나고는 이제 곧 떠나감인가요?
잡아두는 모든 마음 내리고
자유의 맘으로 저 꽃길 따라 걸으며
당신을 맞이하고 보내야지요

언제나 미소로 맞이하고
언제나 꽃빛으로 피어주는 당신을 닮아
비록 떠난 뒤라도
내내 꽃무릇 향기 잃지 않고 살아야지요.

서울문학 등단, 한국문인협회 이사, 국제PEN 한국본부 이사. 박종화 문학상. 시집
삶의 수채화 외 7권 발간

Like the flowers ready to fall
you are going to leave me after having bloomed once inside me?
I know I should let you go in the same way I met you
walking along the path full of red spider lilies with free and good will
putting down all my heart still holding to you

Being like you always having greeted me with a smile,
always having brought forth blossoms to me,
even after the time we can see each other no more
I will live my life, keeping the fragrance of red spider lilies inside me

---

Made literary debut through *Seoul Literature*. Awarded Park Jong-wha Literature Prize from The Korean Writers Association. Published poetry books *Watercolor Painting of Life* and 7 more.

조앵순

소망

성큼 바람이 왔다

뜨거운 더위 헤치고
드넓은 창공 가로질러

온 우주를 돌아

히말라야 안데스 로키산맥
미끄럼 타고 바람 타고 날아서
땅끝 자락 돌아 돌아…

온 천지 좋은 소식 실어

부드럽게 안겨 와
나의 바람이 되었다

우리의 가을바람

아름다운 열매 열릴 거야.

전북 고창 출생. 월간 순수문학 등단. 종로구숭인시문학아카데미 수료. 한국여자신학교.

Cho Aeng-Sun

A Hope

The wind blows with a striding pace

Pushing its way through the heat
Crossing across the boundless sky

Going around the whole universe

Gliding and flying in the winds
Going around and around
Himalayas, Andes Mountains, Rocky Mountains

Carrying all the good news

Coming to me gently
To be my mind

Our autumnal wind will blow

Bearing beautiful fruits

Born in Gochang, Jeonbuk. Made literary debut through *Seonsoo Literature*. graduated from Korea Women's Theology School. Completed Soong-in Poetry Literature Academy

조앵순

독도 관용

별이 지는 자리
어둠이 옷을 갈아입는다
동녘에 찬란한 빛
검푸른 물결 위에 보배로운 섬 하나
언제부턴가 바위로 태어나
외로움 찾아들면 시린 가슴팍
파도에 씻어 보았지
거칠은 바위틈에 생명이 나고
마알간 하늘 먹고 자란
왕호장근 번행초 노란색 애기똥풀
한낮의 평화 새들의 합창
신이 주는 눈부신 선물이라지
칼날같이 거센 폭풍우 이겨내고
목놓아 울던 겨레의 외침소리
갈매기 떼 높은 날갯짓 바람 치면
사랑을 허물 털 듯 이런저런 이야기들
석양 지는 노을빛에 나그네 배 떠나면
독도는 꽃불로 투항하는 가없는 바다를 품는다.

Cho Aeng-Sun

Magnanimity of Dokdo Island

At the place the stars fall
darkness changes its attire
Like the light burning in the east at dawn
a precious island stands on the dark blue waves
Born as a rock in time no one knows when
the island has been enduring biting loneliness
washing the cold heart with ocean waves
Knotweeds, shrubs, yellow celandine flowers
all growing at the cracks in the rocky island
feeding themselves under the clear sky
listening to the peaceful choir of birds
as if being blessed by a divine god
Overcoming the rainstorms raised in the slashing wind
the island stands firm with the roaring outcries for the nation
If tourists leave their stories behind like forsaken love
when their boat takes off like a traveler in the twilight of the sunset
along with the seagulls flying high in the wind
Dokdo Island embraces the ocean in starlight bursting like fireworks

조풍연

피안彼岸 길

속살 뽀얀 겹꽃잎들이
마지막 긴 여운을 남기고
봄바람에 펄펄 휘날리어
미지의 길을 떠나고 있다

다시는 오지 않으리라는
숨결 가득한 피안의 행렬이리라

아니, 나 가거든 잊지 말아달라는
애절한 당부이리라

꽃잎 무덤길에
눈부신 초록 길은 새로 열리고
살면서 아려서 무수히 꽃물들인
눈물 한 방울조차
모두 다 떨구고 가리라는
맑은 영혼의 마지막 몸짓인가보다

Cho Poong-Youn

The Path for Nirvana

Compound petals white in flesh
leaving last long lingering emotions
set out a journey into the unknown
fluttering in the spring wind

They must have joined in a procession
to reach nirvana with no coming back, though

Or, they might be pleading not to forget them
once they have gone forever

For the petals on the way to the graves
a dazzling new path of the green is newly open;
the petals pouring down the last drop of flowery tears
that have been suppressed while they are alive in pain
make their last gesture with the soul pure and innocent
for they would go on the journey leaving everything
behind

조풍연

세월 앞에 서면

자꾸 작아지는 몽당기억으로
닳고 무거워진 세월 앞에 서면

어느 날 문득
낡은 멍석같이 버려지는 건가요

쇠똥구리 같이 달구어 온
붉어진 세월도
한때의 꽃춤일 뿐 멀게만 느껴집니다

언제나 한결같이 온전하고
동백나무처럼 푸를 수는 없는 일이겠죠

소중히 간직했던 추억들조차
영화의 한 장면 같이 저물어
쓱쓱 지워지고 그저 잊혀져갈 뿐인가요

메타빌드 대표/공학박사, 한국SW·ICT총연합회 회장, 제28회 영랑문학상 수상(시집: 화성에서 온 꿈나무 오름), 2023년 순수문학 수필 신인당선작(탱자 꽃, 꿈나무 오름), 2020년 서울문학 시 신인상당선작(세월, 옛집, 등불), 순수문학문인회 이사, 서울문학문인회 부회장, 한국문인협회 회원, 국제펜클럽 회원, 서울사진클럽 자문위원

Cho Poong-Youn

Standing in Front of Time

With the memories getting weaker and smaller
standing in front of time felt heavy and worn out

All of a sudden, I ask myself
if I am an old straw mat that is about to be abandoned

Detached from all the time I have lived through
working hard like a dung beetle
I might be a flower dancing all along in the void

It is not quite possible to keep ourselves
the same and whole as always like the green of camellias

Even the reminiscence cherished and kept in the heart,
being forgotten or erased helplessly in time, would remain
like a scene in the movie getting faded in our memory

CEO of Metabuild, Ph.D. in engineering. President of Korea SW ICT United Society. Made literary as an essayist debut through *Seonsoo Literature* in 2023 and as a poet through *Seoul Literature* in 2020. Member of The Korean Writers association. Awarded The 28th Youngrang Literature Prize. Published poetry book *A Dreaming Tree from Mars*.

주광일

박꽃

사람들 눈에 띄기 싫어

사람들 입에 오르기 싫어

밤에만 살짝 피는 박꽃이여

티 하나 없이 하이얀 꽃잎

맑고 수줍은 여인 같구나

달 없는 밤

별처럼 빛나는 보석이여

오늘 밤엔 아무도 모르게

그대와 함께 단꿈을 꾸고 싶구나

1992년 시집 '저녁노을 속의 종소리'로 시작 활동. 국제 PEN한국본부 회원, 변호사(한국·미국 워싱턴 D.C.) 법학박사, 전 국민고충처리 위원장, 전 서울고등검찰청 검사장, 전 세종대 석좌교수. 서울법대 문우회 회장, 순수 문학상 대상 수상

Chu Kwang-Il

Gourd flower

Unwilling catch the eyes of people,
Unwiilling to be talked about by people,
The gourd flower blooms gently only at night.
Its pure white petals, without a single flaw,
Like a clear and shy maiden.
On a moonlless night,
A jewel shining like a star.
Tonight, unnoticed by anyone,
I wish to dream sweet dreams with you.

주광일

큰눈

모든 것이
거꾸로 되어 버려

뒤죽박죽
엉망진창

숨을 쉴 수가
없게 된 세상은

확 뒤집어야
바로 선다

폭설경보는 없었지만
한밤중 계엄령처럼

큰눈 내려 온 세상을
하얗게 만들듯

Chu Kwang-Il

Heavy Snow

Everything
has turned upside down,

a chaotic mess,
utterly tangled.

A world where breathing
has become impossible

must be flipped over
to stand upright again.

Though no blizzard warning was issued,
like martial law in the dead of night,

heavy snow falls,
blanketing the world in white.

채자경

새해의 기도

남쪽 강 건너온 바람을 찍어
동트는 하늘에 기도문을 쓴다
온누리에 별빛 피어나리라

돌개바람은 밤낮 분간 없이
똘똘 뭉친 음모로
싸움을 부추길 때도
풀들은 몸 일으켜 희망가를 부른다

평화를 잃은 회색 독설들이
자욱하게 몰려오는 새벽
사랑의 편지는 초록 칠판 가득하여라

물빛 하늘 고드름 타고 내려온
꽃바람 봄산에 부는 날
산천 잎들은 볼살을 살찌우리라

Chae Ja-Kyung

A Prayer for the New Year

Dipping into the wind coming across a river in the south
I write a prayer in the sky at dawn
wishing for the starlight to glow all over the world

Even at the time the whirlwind incites conflicts
with all kinds of malevolent conspiracies
spreading rapidly all over the place day and night
grasses, though, raise themselves singing a song of hope

Even at the time biting remarks keeping no faith in peace
rush in like thick fog at menacing dawn
letters of love would be written all over the board in green

On a day in spring, gentle wind blows from the sky
down to the mountains, melting icicles with the scent of flowers;
all the leaves sprouting and growing will gain weight on the cheeks

채자경

어느 시인의 노래

나 바람 따라 구름 따라 걸어요
나 눈을 떠도 나 눈을 감아도 가득한
그리움 속을 걸어요

파란 하늘엔 파란 추억을 그리고요
노을빛 하늘에는 외로움을 그리죠

빛줄기가 들려주는 노래에 하염없이
나는 빗물되어 흘러가요

산그늘도 만나고 개여울을 만나
흐린 날의 침묵을 지우려 해요
한발 가슴에 묻은 왜가리는
외로워서 외발로 선 시인인가요

본명 채경자. 한국문학인상, 시집 목련꽃 사다리

Chae Ja-Kyung

Song of a Poet

I take a walk following the winds and the clouds
Strolling with longing always felt inside me
With my eyes open or closed

In the blue sky, I draw the memories in blue
In the sky at the sunset I draw my loneliness

To the song the streaks of sunlight play
I tune in and flow endlessly like the sunlight

At the mountain shadows and streams I come across
I am going to delete the silence of cloudy days
asking myself if I am a lonely poet standing on one leg
like a gray heron conserving heat tucking one leg into the body

---

Her real name is Chai Kyung-ja. Awarded Korean Writers Prize.
Published poetry book *Magnolia Ladder*

최예찬

할미꽃

머~언 산
외딴 골짜기
허리 굽은 할미꽃
꿈결처럼 왔다 간
햇살 묶음
바람결에 움트는
외로운 마음
달빛 속에 겹겹이 쌓인
그리움의 순간들
세월 속에 묻어 둔
서럽고 서러운 것들이여
그립고 그리운 것들이여

월간 순수문학 등단. 한국문인협회, 국제PEN 회원. 순수문학인협회 상임이사 역임.
시집 '두메 산골' 외

Choi Yea-Chan

Pasqueflower

Far away
in a remote mountain valley
a pasqueflower blooms on the bent stem
in the dazzling sunshine
coming and going like a dream,
in the wind gently blowing
putting forth the lonely mind
All the moments of longing
stacked in the layers of the moonlight
the pasqueflower seems to have buried in time,
all those sorrow
all those yearning desire

Made literary debut through *Seonsoo Literature*. Member of Tthe Korean Writers Association & PEN International, Korea Center. Former standing board member of Seonsoo Literature Association. Published poetry book *Secluded Mountain Village* and more

최예찬

봄봄봄

봄은 다리가 아픈가 봐
나비들을 타고 오는 걸 보면

골짜기 내를 건너
오두막 마당을 질러

누렁황소의 등을 타고
타박타박 걸어온다네

진달래 향기에 취해
보내는 마음이 아파

잠시 머뭇거리다가
느슨하게 뻗은 기차길 따라

소로길 논밭을 지나
한들한들 아지랑이 타고 남으로 온다네

왜 그렇게 늦니
지지배배 종달새 종알대고

Choi Yea-Chan

Spring Coming All Over The Places

Spring seems to feel pain in legs
It always comes taking a ride of butterfly wings

Crossing the stream of a valley
Cutting across the front yard of a cabin

Riding on a bull's back
It comes taking a step one by one

Being intoxicated in the scent of azalea flowers
Feeling sorry for the time to go

Lingering a little while
but again following the railroad stretched loosely

Passing the narrow paths of rice fields
Spring comes to the south along with shimmering haze

While skylarks are chirping a tune
Complaining at the spring arriving a little late

최외득

맞바람

바깥바람이 무섭더냐
마음 안에서 부는 바람이 더한 두려움이다

흔들리며 살아서 고달프다면
저 들판의 꽃인들 며칠을 살겠는가

우리에겐 좋은 뿌리를 가지지 않았더냐
두 팔을 벌리면 큰 의지가 되는데

우리여, 벼랑에 선 나무가 될 텐가
우리가 바람 잡는 숲이 될 터인가

시인, 소설가, 문학평론가. 한국문인협회 사무총장. 한국소설가협회 이사. 계간문학저널문인회 회장. 시집 『껍질을 가진 나무는 얼지 않는다』 『반듯한 보도블록』 『행복한 하루 살기』 소설집 『월식 인간』 한국노총위원장 표창. 행정안전부장관 표창. 옥조근정훈장. 제15회 영랑문학상 우수상, 제10회 한국문협서울시문학상(소설부문), 2021 문학저널창작문학상(소설부문) 수상.

Choi Woe-Deuk

Headwind

The wind blowing inside the mind is more scary
than the wind blowing outside

How long do the flowers wavering in the field survive
if they think their lives wearisome?

We have our life firmly rooted in good soil
and the strong arms to support ourselves

It's all up to us whether we are going to be
a tree standing on the cliff or a forest catching the
wind

최외득

동백꽃

그토록 가슴 저미는 기도

동박새 울음에
명쾌한 얼음이란

사랑이라면
저녁 하늘처럼
눈감을 줄 알아야지

눈을 감는 건
극복의 의지가 아니겠느냐

외로우니까
눈감은 하늘에서
별이 총총하지 않느냐

울어서 가다듬는 애절한 목소리가
붉게 물들어서
그토록 깊이 외롭고 싶은 것이겠지

Choi Woe-Deuk

Camellia Flowers

A prayer breaking the heart bitterly

The cries of warbling white-eyes
Manifesting a crystal clear truth

Real love
Teaching how to close the eyes
Like the evening sky

Closing the eyes
Signifying the will to overcome

With the eyes closed in loneliness
The stars glow brightly
In the sky at night

Appearing to have the doleful voice
Coming out of the throat cleared and turning red
Longing to be in loneliness so deeply felt in the heart

최철훈

광음(光陰)

퐁!
연못 속으로
돌멩이 하나가 빠졌다.

방금,
그 돌멩이는 누구일까?
돌멩이일까?

충남 천안 생. 고려대학교(심리학). 경희대학교(석사 경영학). 노동부 선임 연구원. 대한경제 연구원 수석 연구위원. 한국적성 연구소장. 육군소령 전역. 순수문학 등단. 백두산 문학 신인상(2014). 순수문학 신인상(2019)

Choi Cheul-Hoon

The Fleeting Light and Shadow

Pong!

The one pebble dropped into the lake.
Who could that it have been
just now?

Could it be a pebble?

최철훈

정을 쪼다

살아가면서,
하나를 하면 하나를 못하고
하나를 못하면 하나를 하네

하나를 하여, 하나를 못하고
하나를 못하여, 하나를 하니
둘은 서로 하나일세

하고 못함이 없는 하나이니
하나를 해도, 못해도 하나일세

뙤약볕 아래
노(老)석수장이가 하루 종일 정을 쪼네

Choi Cheul-Hoon

To Carve with Care

As we go through life,
when I do one thing, I can't do another.
when I can't do one thing,
I end up doing another.

By dping one, I can't do the other.
By not doing one,
I end up doing the other.
And thus, both are one.

Doing or not doing makes no difference:
Whether I succeed or fail,
It is still one.

Under the blistering sun,
the old stone sculptor chips away
at his work all day long.

추정희

향기에 취해

어느 가슴 그리움으로
산기슭에 홀로 섰는가
키 큰 아카시나무

흰나비 무리지어 모여 살듯
하얀 꽃자루 달고
달콤한 향 사뿐히 흔들며
내려왔다 사라지고 다시 오는

지난밤
봄 밤 설친 내 님
꽃잎 누운 자리에
눈물보다 깊은 숨결
뿌려 놓았나

바람에 흩날리는 향기
그대가 되어
세상 가득 그리움으로
출렁이면
그대 속에 나 흠뻑 취하네

Chu Jeong-Hee

Intoxicated in the Scent

Alone in the mountain slope
with longing in the heart
stands a tall acacia tree

As if white butterflies live in a swarm
white penduncles of flowers in cluster sway
scattering sweet scent lightly
coming down, vanishing, and coming back again

In the spring night
my love who has interrupted sleep
comes out dispersing the breath deeper than tears
on the ground acacia petals are lying

With the scent floating in the wind
becoming you, my love,
making the world undulate
with my desperate longing
I would get fully intoxicated in love for you

추정희

춘분

나풀나풀
나비의 몸에서 초록 내 물씬
첫 나들이인가
꽃봉오리 싹 틔우기 좋은 날
작은 너의 몸짓에 마음 설렌다
진화하지 못해 땅 속에서 사산한
이름 없는 생명처럼 잠자던 너
털복숭이 애벌레로 풀섶 그늘에 숨어
꿈틀대던 변천을 거듭한 너를 보고
하루 온통 설렛다
춘분에 흰나비 훨훨
초록 내 물씬
첫 나들이인가 보다

전남 광주 출생. 숭의여대 문예창작과 졸업. 2008년 월간 순수문학 신인상 등단. 한국문인협회 회원. 전국 창작시 동상. 서울 마포 신문사 여성 백일장 우수상외다수. 창포시 동인지. 공간외다수 동인지. 일성 문학회 부회장

Chu Jeong-Hee

Spring Equinox

Flapping their wings
butterflies evoking green so fresh
for the first outing in spring
on a great day for flower buds to sprout
making my mind flutter with your gestures
You have been in sleep like an unknown life
having failed to evolve but found dead in the soil
until you start to develop yourself hiding in the shade
as a hairy larva wriggling and growing,
and I feel so good all day long feeling my heart flutter
White butterflies flit on the day of spring equinox
evoking green so fresh and natural
for the first outing in spring

하재룡

라일락꽃 피면

4월이 오면
동숭동 마로니에공원
라일락꽃 핀다

반독재 외치던
분노의 젊은 함성
미라보 다리 건너고

시국과 사랑 인생을
논하던 선술집의 밤
깊어 가는데

라일락꽃 향과 함께
청춘들의 사랑도
익어 간다

라일락꽃 피면
떠오르는
젊은 날의 추억
아, 잔인한 계절이여

Ha Jai-Ryong

If Lilacs bloom

When April comes
At Marronnier park in Dongsung-dong
Lilacs bloom

Crying out against dictatorship
Young people roared in rage
Marching as if crossing Le Pont Mirabeau

The night grew late
At the pub we debated
On politics, love, and life

With the scents of lilacs blooming
Love of the youths
Grew ripe

When lilacs bloom
Past memories finds me in fleeting moments
Ah, how cruel it is for a season

하재룡

웅얼웅얼 찔레꽃 노래

어머니는
노래를 못 하시는 줄 알았다

한번도
노래하는 모습
뵌 적이 없었으므로

요양병원에 누워계실 때
망연히 혼자 웅얼웅얼 거리시던
찔레꽃 노래

아, 아 어머니는
정말 노래를 못 하시는 줄 알았다

세상에서 가장 아름답게 울려오던
웅얼웅얼 찔레꽃 노래
지금도 마음 저 깊은 곳, 떠돌고 있다.

전북 남원 출신. 서울대 문리대 졸업, 전북대 행정학 박사. 월간 순수문학 등단(2020년), 순수문학상 작가대상(2021년) 수상. 시집 『라일락 꽃 피면』 외 다수. 현) 순수문학 이사, 필동인, 남원문인협회, 한국문인협회, 국제PEN 회원

Ha Jai-Ryong

Mumbling a Song 'Baby Rose'

I didn't know
that my mother could sing a song

Not even once
I haven't seen her
singing a song

Until I saw her lying alone
on the sick bed at a nursing hospital
vacantly mumbling a song 'Baby Rose'

Ah, I really haven't thought about my mother
being able to sing any song

'Baby Rose,' the most beautiful song in the world
my mother was mumbling, still resonates in my ear,
circulating around at the bottom of my heart

Graduated from Seoul National Univ. Ph. D. in public administration from Jeonbuk Univ. Made literary debut through *Seonsoo Literature* in 2020. Member of PEN International, Korea Center & Board member of Seonsoo Literature Association. Awarded Seonsoo Literature Prize in 2021. Published poetry book *If Lilacs Bloom* and many more

한민서

제자리

한걸음 한걸음 나아가다 보면
지금보다는 괜찮겠지
한참을 걸었다 아무 생각없이
나의 눈은 땅을 향하고
나의 발은 목적지도 없이 어딘가를 향해
한걸음 한걸음…

아… 여기는 어디인가 나는 누구인가
방황하는 나의 다리를 보며
두려움이 찾아왔다

가만히 서서 눈을 감고
천천히 숨을 내쉴 때 그제서야 보이는
파란 하늘에 뭉게구름
둥실둥실 흩날리는 구름을 보며
나는 내 자신을 내려 놓는다

흘러가는 구름처럼
나 또한 흐르는 바람에 몸을 맡긴다.

Han Min-Seo

The Same Place

Taking a step farther, one by one,
Thinking about the better future
Walking for a while absentmindedly
Staring down the earth
Following my footsteps advancing without a destination
One step at a time

Ah… Wondering where I am and who I am
Looking down at my feet wandering
Feeling fear inside me

Pausing still, standing with my eyes closed
Breathing out, I finally see
The cumulus in the blue sky
Looking up lightly floating scattered clouds
I put myself down

Like the clouds drifting away
I give myself to the wind

한민서

컴퓨터 자판기

컴퓨터 자판을 두드리고 있다
어제도, 오늘도, 지금 이 순간도
손가락 길이 때문인가
아니면 손가락마다 힘이 달라서 일까
두드릴 때마다 각 다른 소리를 낸다
아무 생각 없이 자판을 치고 있다가도
탁탁 소리 때문에 나도 모르게 리듬을 타게 된다
마치 피아노 연주를 하는 것 마냥
어떨 땐 빠르게 어느 시점에는 느리게
손을 움직이다 보면
어느새 마지막 마침표를 찍을 순간
타자 연습을 하던 때가 있었는데
이제는 열 손가락이 제법 빠르게 움직인다.

월간 순수문학 시 등단. 한림대학교 국어국문학과 졸업. 한국문인협회 회원. 필 동인 회원. 제33회 세계시인대회 고려문학상. 제50회 문예춘추 신인문학상. 제47회 한민족통일문예제전 경기도지사상. 영랑문학 우수상 수상

Han Min-Seo

Computer Keyboard

I am typing on the computer keyboard
Yesterday, today, even right at this moment
I hear different sounds from the keyboard
whenever I type, making me wonder
if my fingers, weak or strong, make different sounds
While tying on the keyboard mechanically
I find myself getting into the rhythm of a sort
as if I enjoy playing the piano
with my fingers moving fast sometimes
or slowly some other times
until I finally get to the end with a period
Back in the days I used to practice my typing skill
but not any more, for I am quite good at typing now

Made literary debut through *Seonsoo Literature*. Graduated from Hallym Univ. majoring in Korean literature. Member of The Korean Writers Association. Member of coterie Phil. Awarded the 50th prize of New Writer from Munye Choonchoo, Youngrang Literature Prize.

한현삼

환희

1
연초록 빛을따라
꽃소식 스미는가

훈풍에 염원실은
청아한 목련화냐

겨우내
응축한 순결
님의 미소 이어라.

2
햇살에 물이들어
봄향기 너울대나

산하를 알록달록
연분홍 진달래야

빛 고운
실바람 타고
그대 품에 갈거나.

Han Hyun-Sam

Joy

1
Following the green shimmering light
Tidings of flowers come permeating the air

Elegant magnolia flowers bloom
In the warm breeze carrying our wishes

After being suppressed all winter long
They finally bloom revealing their purity
Like a smile of my love

2
Tinged in the sunlight
The scent of spring spreads lightly

Azalea flowers bloom in light purple
Painting all the mountains with colorful hues

Riding on the light wind
dancing with the beautiful sunlight
I wish I could run into your arms

한현삼

비 - 7

그 때
그 추억
간절했나

새벽 녘
요란하다
솔솔 내리치는
빗 방울
창을 흔든다

강 건너
멀고 먼 길
무얼 찾아 왔다더냐

꽃 나비
시샘하여
그냥
자랑 삼아 오는건가……

월간 순수문학 시 등단. 단국대학교 졸업. 한양대학교 대학원 졸업. 명예인문학박사. 한국문인협회 회원. 필동인 회원. 타쉬켄트 국제비엔날레 심사위원 및 예술감독. 우즈베키스탄 예술아카데미 최고상"골드메달"수상. 한국신미술협회 이사장. 대한민국신미술대전 조직위원장

Han Hyun-Sam

Rain-7

Longing for
The time going back
In memories

At dawn
Making loud sounds
Raindrops fall
Hitting and shaking
The window

I wonder what they are looking for
Coming from far away
After crossing the rivers

Perhaps
Coming to show off themselves
Feeling jealous of butterflies flying around flowers

Made literary debut through *Seonsoo Literature*. Graduated from Dankook Univ and Hanyang Univ. Graduate School. Honorary Ph. D. in humanities. Member of The Korean Writers Association. Judging committee member and art director of Tashkent International Biennale. Awarded The Gold Medal from Art Academy in Uzbekistan. President of Korea New Fine Art Association.

홍경자

일을 하는 마음

함께 일하자는 초대를 받으면
고마워서 신바람 나게
옆 사람 흉내도 내며 열심히 일한다

업무에 익숙해지면서
재미가 없어지고 싫증이 나도 하라는 대로 한다
불이익을 받을까 두려워서…

이왕이면 나와 내 가족의 밥줄인
고용주에게 잘 보이려 그의 뜻 헤아리며
즐겁게 일하자고 힘겨워하는 몸과 마음 추스린다

가볍고 기쁜 마음으로 정성을 다하다 보면
행복한 일꾼으로 새롭게 태어나
주인의 진정한 협력자 친구가 된다

Hong Kyung-Ja

The Mind at Work

When hired to work together
people do their best in their line of work
being thankful while learning the work

After getting accustomed to the work
they feel bored but do what they were told to do
being afraid of getting disadvantaged at work

Workers often think their livelihoods depend on their boss,
so they try to make good impressions on the employer
thinking positively and cheering themselves up

While doing their best with happy thought and sound mind
workers gradually get satisfaction from their job
becoming not just a worker but a real friend of the employer

홍경자

초록빛 은행낙엽

이상기온에 볼품없는 가을 색깔
아쉬운 마음에
지난해를 떠올리며 새해에 기대를 걸어보네

설상가상 갑작스런 강풍에
나뭇잎들이 우수수
시퍼런 은행나무 잎들이 길가에 쌓여가네

노란 물 들여 보지도 못하고 떨어지다니…
안쓰러운 마음에 떠오르는 것은
어린 자식 먼저 떠나보낸 어미의 마음이네

2009 월간순수문학 등단. 2021년 PEN문학상 등 수상. 시집 『내 삶에는 울림이 있는가』 외 다수

Hong Kyung-Ja

Ginkgo Leaves in Green

With autumnal hues looking poor in unusual temperature
I feel wistful recalling beautiful tinged leaves of last year
and take a walk now hoping for great autumn next year

In the gusty wind blowing all of a sudden
the leaves often rustle down
and I see ginkgo leaves fallen in green lying on the ground

For the ginkgo leaves having fallen before they turn yellow
I feel sorry watching them wither on the roadside,
as if I am a mother who has to bury her young child in her heart

---

Made literary debut through *Seonsoo Literature* in 2009. Awarded PEN Literature Prize in 2021 and more. Published poetry book *What is Resonating in My Life* and more

홍금희

첫눈 오는 날

첫눈은 소리 없이 내린다
그것도
일 년 만에

첫눈 오는 날엔
어디선가
꼭
연락이 올것 같아
설레인다

멀리
타국으로 간 막내아들
영영 소식 없던 그 어떤 사람에게서

창문을 열고
밖을 내다본다
첫눈을 마중하러

나뭇잎 한 두 잎 매달린
나뭇가지 위에

Hong Geum-Hee

On the Day the First Snow Falls

The first snow falls in silence
As it always does
Every year

On the day the first snow falls
I feel my heart fluttering
Expecting for sure
I would get a call or a greeting
From someone or somewhere

Probably
From the youngest son of mine living abroad
Or someone I lost touch with for a long time

Through the open window
I look outside
Greeting the first snow falling

On a leaf or two hanging
At the twigs

도시의 회색빛 지붕 위에

세상의 모든 것을
하얗게 덮는다

이제
남은 것은 나의 맘

첫눈이
오는 날엔

모두를
사랑하게 된다

제주 서귀포 출생. 제주대학교를 졸업. 월간 순수문학 등단. 뉴스엔제주 1회 여성 백일장 장려상 수상. 현재 노인 사회복지사로 활동 중

Over the gray rooftop of the city

The first snow covers
Everything in white

Now
What is left is my mind

On the day
The first snow falls

I fall in love with everyone

Made literary debut through *Seonsoo Literature*. Graduated from Jeju Univ. Currently, social worker for the elderly. Awarded the prize at the 1st New and Jeju Women's Writing Contest.

홍금희

팥죽 한 그릇

야, 야, 창 창 창
문 두드리는 소리

세찬 바람 속
아침 식사하라네

쟁반에
가득 담긴
팥죽 한 그릇

안 집 구부정한
할머니는
새벽 팥죽을 쑤시고

동네
이 집 저 집
정을 나누러 다닌다

Hong Geum-Hee

A Bowl of Red Bean Porridge

Bang, bang, bang
The sound of hitting the door

In a strong wind
hollering at me to take a breakfast

Holding
a bowl of red bean porridge
on a tray

A stooped old lady
living in the main house
makes red bean porridge at dawn

To deliver what she prepared
she visits the neighbors here and there
sharing her affectionate mind with them

빈 그릇 드리지 못하여
준비해 둔
떡국을 드렸다

어젯밤,
팥죽 먹고
한라산 눈꽃 축제를
걸어 두었는데

눈 뜨니
걸어 둔 생각이
열매 맺어
신기하기만 하다

동지 팥죽 한 그릇에
한해 동안
아팠던 마음들이
사르르
떠나간다

Receiving the porridge
I give her a rice cake soup in return
as a token of my appreciation

Last night
after eating the red bean porridge
I spent sometime thinking about
'Snowdrop Festival at Mountain Halla'

In this morning when I woke up
I was surprised to find
that my thoughts bear some fruit

Over a bowl of red bean porridge
I see all the troubles
that have been hurting me
for a year long
disappear as if melting away

홍영숙

봄날의 조우

한파 몰아치는 겨울
인적 드문 공원길
백합 수선화 꽃무릇 팻말이
보이는 수목정원을 지나다
발길을 멈췄다

앙상한 나뭇가지 아래
층층이 덮여있는
바싹 마른 낙엽들 틈새에
햇살에 반짝이는 초록 잎들

새 생명을 싹틔우기 위해
생의 마지막을 포근한 이불이
되어준 듯 따뜻해지던 마음

삼월의 봄날 꽃은 피지 않았으나
튼실하게 올라온 진초록 잎들
낙엽 품에 안겨 반겨준다

Hong Young-Sook

An Encounter of a Spring Day

During a cold snap in the late winter
I walk on a remote parkway
and stop by a forest garden
with a designated area sign
for the burgeoning lilies and daffodils

Under the tree branches thin and bare
fallen dry leaves are lying
covering the ground in layers
with burgeoning new leaves shining in the sunlight

Fallen leaves become comfortable blankets
to keep the buds alive with the warm heart
in order to bring forth new lives

On a spring day in March too early for flowers to bloom
fallen leaves happily embrace
the new sprouting leaves growing well and fresh

홍영숙

탄천의 물 소리

봄 햇살에 반짝이며
소리 없이 흐르는 물 소리
물길 속에 비쳐지는
물구나무 선 나무들
한폭의 수묵화다

흘러가다 미끄러지듯
하얀 포말을 일으키며
커지는 물 소리

다시 결 고운 고요함

징검다리 부드럽게 돌아가며
평화를 노래한다

흐르는 물이 되어
살아가라는 울림의 소리

순수문학 등단, 영랑문학상 본상. 시집 「곡선의 미학」 외 2권

Hong Young-Sook

The Sounds of Water Flowing at Tancheon

With the sounds of water flowing silently
glittering in the spring sunlight
trees standing upside down
in the reflection on the surface of the stream
present an ink-and-wash painting

The sounds of water are getting louder
when the water creates white foam
while flowing and sliding

Again moving with the ripples in tranquility

Softly turning around the stepping stones
the water sings for peace

Asking us to live like water
always flowing in peace

Made literary debut through *Seonsoo Literature*. Awarded Youngrang Literature Prize. Published poetry book *Aesthetics of a Curve* and 2 more.

홍은숙

무덤

어머니 자궁을 떠나
긴 고행 끝에
돌아온 고향

한 세월
부서지도록 열심히 일도 해 보고
이곳저곳 구석구석 여행도 해 보고
애간장 다 타도록
미워하며
사랑하며 살아온 세상

얼룩지고 더께 진 상처 자국
아쉬움과 허망한 그림자

얼마나
사는 것이 힘들었으면
하나같이
둥글게 둥글게 무던한 걸 원했을까

Hong Eun-Sug

Graves

Since having left mother's womb
It took so long to return to hometown
After suffering hardships

For a life time
Working so hard enough to feel burnout
Traveling around every possible place
Feeling anxious all the time
Hating or loving somebody
So would the dead have lived

Having scars got thickened and discolored
With the shadowy feeling of regret and emptiness

I wonder how tough their lives had been
For they have their own grave now
With a half-round shape

얼마나
사는 것이 어지러웠으면
홀로 외딴곳
호젓한 쓸쓸함을 택했을까

충북보은. 1996년 순수문학 등단. 한국문인협회, 국제펜 한국본부, 여주문인협회 회원. 국제PEN 경기지역 사무국장 역임. 여주문인협회 지부장 역임. 시집 '강가에 앉아' 1~4집. 제16회 영랑문학상, 제8회 유주현문학상 향토상, 경기예술 대상, 여주시민상 수상.

Asking myself how confused they had felt
Living a life that makes them prefer now
Staying in loneliness
All alone at a remote place

Made literary debut through *Seonsoo Literature* in 1996. Member of The Korean Writers Association, PEN International, Korea Center, & Yoeju Writers Association. Former director of PEN International, Kyunggi province. Published poetry book Sitting by the River vol.1 to vol. 4. Awarded The 16th Youngrang Literature Prize, Thte 8th Yoo Ju-hyun Literature Prize, Kyunggi Art Grand Prize.

홍은숙

등산

세상일 잊고자
나는
산으로 가는데
세상일 돌보고자
바람은
산 아래 마을로 간다

청청한 나무의 정기를 타고
골짜기
골짜기
정갈한 향기를 거두어
지천으로 쌓인 만고풍상
얽히고
설키고
상처 난 뒤에야 깨달은 이치
용서하며
사랑하려
세상으로 간다

Hong Eun-Sug

Climbing Mountains

In order to forget
The worldly matters of daily life
I go up to the mountains;
In order to take care of
The worldly matters
The wind comes down to the village

Carrying the spirits of green trees
Down to the valleys
Down to the valleys
Collecting the fragrance clean and fresh
Going through the hardships all around
Being tangled
Being twisted
Getting so many hurts
With a wisdom to spread
Of how to forgive and love
The wind comes down from the mountains

어리석은 나는
나 자신을 구원하고자
산으로 가는데
못미더운 세상 돌보고자
바람은
산 아래 마을로 간다

In order to save
Me being too foolish
I climb up the mountains;
The wind comes down to the villages
To take care of worldly matters
Still unsettled and untrustworthy

미래를 빛낼 시인들의 국영문 시선집

朴永河 외 58인 지음
김인영 번역

2025. 6. 15. 초판
2025. 6. 25. 발행

발행처 · 순수문학사
출판주간 · 朴永河
등 록 제2-1572호

서울 중구 퇴계로48길 11 협성BD 202호
TEL (02) 2277-6637~8
FAX (02) 2279-7995
E-mail ; seonsookr@hanmail.net

· 저자와의 합의하에 인지를 생략함
· 잘못된 책은 바꾸어 드립니다

ISBN 979-11-91153-82-8

가격 20,000원